SOFT NUT BIKE TOUR OF BURMA

EXPLORING THE LESS TRAVELLED ROADS OF MYANMAR

TRACY STANLEY

LES STANLEY

Copyright © Tracy Stanley and Les Stanley have asserted their rights under the Copyright, Design & Patents Act 1988 to be identified as the authors of this work.

All rights reserved. No part of this publication may be reproduced, or transmitted by any person or entity (including Google, Amazon or similar organisations), in any form or by any means electronic or mechanical, including photocopying, recording, scanning or by any information storage and retrieval system or transmitted in any form, or by any means without the prior written permission without prior permission in writing from the publisher.

A CIP catalogue record for this book is available from the National Library of Australia.

Paperback
ISBN-13: 978-0-6486607-5-0

Front cover photo taken at Banana Mountain by Tracy
Cover Design by Nabinkarna on Fiverr

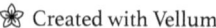 Created with Vellum

CONTENTS

Map of Myanmar	v
Advance Praise for Soft Nut Bike Tour	1

PART I

Prologue	5
Dedication	9
Why Soft Nut Bike Tour of Burma?	10
Pain in the back (Les)	14
Bye bye Brisbane	17
Bustling Bangkok	20

PART II

Border Town - Mae Sot	47
Crossing the frontier	51
Majestic mountains - Hpa An	59
Hpa An to Mawlamyine	65
Mawlamyine	73
Mawlamyine to Thanbyuzayat	77
Thanbyuzayat to Ye	83
Ye to Bin Le Wa	89
Ye to San Hlan	95
San Hlan to Dawei	99
Dawei to Huay Plu	105

PART III

Reflecting on the journey	115
Best bits	116
Biggest challenges	125
Words describing our leader	131
Planning a cycling trip in Burma	133
Acknowledgments	139
About Tracy Stanley	141

About Les Stanley	144
About Hidden Holiday House	147
Favourite foods and snacks	151
References and further reading	155
Photos from the tour	159

MAP OF MYANMAR

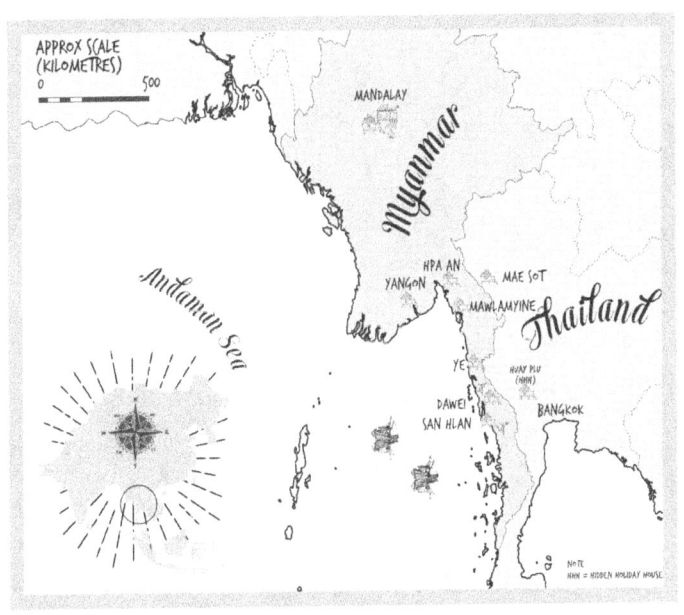

ADVANCE PRAISE FOR SOFT NUT BIKE TOUR

I'm still nervous every time they head off with Chris to these remote places. However, I thoroughly enjoyed reading Tracy and Les' diary of the trip.

Gwen McCullough (Tracy's mother)

PART I

BRISBANE TO BANGKOK

PROLOGUE

A river of salty sweat mixed with sun cream was leeching painfully into my eyes, I blinked furiously but to no avail. Eventually, not for the first time that day, I dismounted from my bike and reached for the grubby, green sweat towel clamped on my bike rack. The suffering was exacerbated because I was also three days into a cold. I reassured myself that I had not caught the dreaded Corona virus which was wreaking havoc in Wuhan, China and causing widespread panic around the world and most particularly at my parent's house who could not understand why, at the age of 56, I had decided to go on a bike trip in Southern Myanmar.

I was four days into the Soft Nut Bike Tour of Burma which was being undertaken during the laughably misnamed cool season. South-East Asia has three official seasons; the hot, the cool and the wet. These are often referred to by visiting foreigners as the hot, the very hot and the so hot my shorts are melting. I was travelling in the cool season so it was just hot and horribly humid from ten o'clock each morning until four pm each afternoon.

The air was smoky making breathing difficult, even for those without a potentially contagious, possibly fatal, lung disease. The bumpy roads were rattling my bike and my resolution to cycle all the way. Chris, our fearless leader, had the uncanny ability to conjure up *chicken-out* options from pretty much anywhere and for pretty much any situation ranging from sickness to laziness. These included a truck or tuk tuk to transport us to the next destination in relative comfort to a hotel of some description and maybe a hot shower. I cleared my nasal passages, remounted the bike and decided to soldier on.

This book describes our journey by bike, train and boat from Mae Sot to Huay Plu via Myanmar, a country of towering temples, wonderfully dressed women and inquisitive children on the Soft Nut Bike Tour of Burma. I say 'our' to include the cohort of ten who comprised the multi-nation cycling group. As will be revealed, a sudden debilitating back spasm pre-departure, meant my husband Les was unable to join us. He did however keep in regular contact by Facebook Messenger and updated his own diary throughout the journey. His reflections are sprinkled throughout this retelling of our expedition.

This book also describes the planning for the trip and the start of the journey from Brisbane to Bangkok. If you've bought this book just to read about the bike trip in Myanmar then I would suggest you go directly to Part 2, to the start of the *Soft Nut* journey in Mae Sot.

DEDICATION

We dedicate this book to Chris Jedrzycki our fearless and redoubtable leader on the Soft Nut Bike Tour of Burma

WHY SOFT NUT BIKE TOUR OF BURMA?

Les and I met Chris and Areeya shortly after arriving in Thailand in 2008. We'd been keen to identify somewhere in the countryside, no more than an hour from Bangkok, where we could escape the hectic city life and take our beloved bikes for an occasional spin. Les found Hidden Holiday House through Google and we knew from our first visit, that this beautiful house on the river, just outside of Huay Plu, would be our go-to place.

It was during one of our many visits that Chris mentioned that he was organising a bike trip along the border between Thailand and Laos with a few of his other regular guests.

'Would you be interested in coming along?' Chris asked.

'Sure', we replied, and that was the beginning of our adventures with a collection of once-a-year cycling friends from around the world, who would visit locations across Thailand, Laos, Cambodia, China and Malaysia during the very short 'cool' season.

I'm not sure how long Myanmar, or Burma as it was previously known during British rule, had been on Chris' potential trip list. We were interested to visit this country that had only opened up completely to tourists in 2012, allowing them to enter for up to a month. Previously, tourists were only allowed to visit major tourist sites on a one week visa. It was particularly attractive that we were visiting areas outside the main cities of Yangon (previously called Rangoon) and Mandalay. From previous trips, Chris knew that the *Baby Boomer* members of his cycling community, preferred shorter cycling days and more frequent stops. So he created two tours.

Participants on the *Tough Nut Tour* of Burma needed to be able to ride 100 kilometres a day with few refreshment breaks. Those on the gentler, *Soft Nut Tour*, would need to be fit enough to ride 60 kilometres over greatly-varying terrain, and would be allowed frequent stops to consume iced coffee and to allow the blood to return to their numbed posteriors. For his older clientele, Chris had come to understand the specific sleeping, showering and bathroom needs so took this in to account when undertaking the scouting trip in order to identify suitable routes and places to rest our heads at night.

. . .

The 2020 cohort for the Soft Nut Tour comprised ten people from seven nationalities. (Chris's wife Areeya was a late and very welcome inclusion to the troupe.)

French - 3
Thai - 2
Canadian - 1
Malaysian - 1
Taiwanese - 1
English - 1
Australian - 1

As a result of our mixed nationalities, there were numerous languages spoken at any time including English, French, Thai and Chinese. I had no problem with English (obviously) and made use of my conversational French and limited Thai, mainly when checking the spiciness of food, 'Mai Phet Ka', (not too spicy please).

All of us were alumni of at least one of Chris' previous tours through the back roads of Asia. This was important as there was a need to be disciplined in getting our panniers packed and bikes on the road early, to take advantage of the cool riding hours in the morning while recognising that things happen, like saddles splitting and brakes breaking, which required extra time. Chris possesses an inborn hatred of the smoothest roads which means we visit villages not often seen, which is wonderful but our bikes may suffer as a result. There was also an underlying ethos of helping each other out and taking turns to ride at the back to ensure that no-one got left behind.

We were aged between 49 and 71 with one participant celebrating his 50th birthday en route. Unfortunately, he spent most of his birthday in bed with a stomach bug recovering from a dodgy food choice at the night market the previous evening.

Our troupe was of course not complete without Les, my husband who unfortunately had had a back incident three weeks prior to departure. I'll leave it to him to share his story.

PAIN IN THE BACK (LES)

A superheated knife is being pushed into your lower back, simultaneously a giant hand is clasping your flesh and squeezing tighter, ever tighter. Blazing spikes impale you. You have no idea how long this pain will last. In reality its duration is one or two seconds but in your mind an eternity passes before temporary respite comes. As you sense a new wave of agony about to assail you, you cry out pathetically *"NO, NO"*, convinced that if you plead sufficiently your willpower can make it stop. The pain is unheeding, it has no concept of sympathy. Eventually, in its own time, it subsides and you breathe deeply, relishing the temporary relief before it grabs at you again, unyielding, impervious to your pleas to cease the torment.

The paramedics arrived as I was writhing and wailing pathetically and I hoped in vain for a magic shot directly into the spot which the devil himself had chosen to spawn his evil offspring. No such luck. They gave me a green plastic tube on which, they told me, I should inhale to relieve the agony. It did nothing, apart from make me cough. They loaded me into their vehicle and we bounced through the Brisbane streets to the hospital as I continued to whimper and rant.

On arrival at the hospital my wife began to answer the standard registration questions; name, date of birth, phone number. She hesitated slightly when asked about any religious affiliation, "none" I yelled out between contortions from my trolley. Why would any form of deity make me suffer like this, to what end? Methodically I ingested various drugs in an effort to quell the pain. Nothing worked. I was told to breathe through it and think of the colour blue. Useless, although I did appreciate the importance of breathing. Yelping like a wounded lion and repeatedly screeching expletives helped a little. Scans were done to eliminate causes such as kidney stones and, to my mind the most likely scenario, an alien presence. "It's just muscle strain, very common," they said as I was wheeled into short stay emergency.

Time passed slowly. The attacks became less frequent. Bedridden, I'd been attempting to relieve my ever-filling bladder into an oddly shaped bottle but, no matter which position I painfully assumed, gravity and physiology failed to achieve the required result. I was fast coming to terms with the necessity of having a catheter inserted when nurse Saint Sarah appeared with a far less drastic solution. A wheelchair with a toilet seat attached. Once I was on the chair Saint Sarah simply wheeled me to the privacy of a nearby bathroom, positioned me with great precision and left me to attain my personal, beatific nirvana. "Just press the button when you're finished," she said, as she floated away on a cloud. Boundless joy filled my soul.

So, *cutting to the chase,* as I know that you did not buy this book to read the intricacies of my unexpected hospital sojourn, I recovered with the help of physiotherapy along with a new exercise regime and was released into my wife's occasionally tender care. The doctor advised that it was probably not a great idea to go cycling in Myanmar at this time. So, like your good self, I followed the journey from the comfort of my sofa. I also kept a diary, so it felt a bit like I was there. I recognise that I'm no Samuel Peyps, but thought you might enjoy my musings which will be sprinkled throughout my wife's reminiscences. (Samuel Pepys was an administrator of the navy of England and Member of Parliament in the 17th century who is most famous for his detailed diary).

BYE BYE BRISBANE
25 JANUARY 2020

Departure day was a strange day. It was weird to arrive at the airport and to see dozens of people wearing masks. I'm heading off at a time of the Corona virus and while at this stage, it doesn't seem to have the epic proportions of the SARS or the MERS virus, everyone is nervous, particularly my mother.

I was delighted by the super easy check in. No longer do you need to fill in security forms or constantly show your passport at Brisbane airport. I sailed through and enjoyed my time reading in the departure lounge. I'd given myself $20 to spend at the airport which I thought would get me a cup of coffee, and two magazines. I was therefore surprised to see that a copy of The Economist and Times, still cost me $19. It was lucky that Les had paid for my coffee and biscuits before I left. I was pleased that I'd bought an empty water bottle and refilled at the airport. So I'm still on track with my budget. I've carefully calculated expenditure for every day with a few treats built in as well. This has been a life-long habit which I acquired from my Dad, who was a careful spender.

I'm also hoping on this trip, apart from being able to survive each of the 60 kilometre bike rides each day, to try and lose some weight. So definitely no alcohol and I need to keep off ice creams and sugary drinks. It's the Nescafe cold-brew drinks that are particularly difficult to avoid when you're on the road because they're so delicious (and cold).

The plane was fairly empty, with only 20% of all seats filled. Even better, there were no screens enclosed in the back of everyone's chairs, which can be particularly annoying if the person seated behind you wants to play a game that involves frequent screen pressing. Everyone wanted to sleep, which was encouraged by the crew pulling down all the shades immediately upon departure. Many passengers had a row to themselves. There was a baby crying somewhere over to the left of me, but it finally settled and so did I.

I was pleased to have picked up a lovely Billabong shirt from one of the Duty-Free shops at the airport. It looked great and could possibly help with in placement advertising in my book if this memoir takes off. I'm on the lookout for partnership opportunities. I also like it because it's such a distinctively Australian brand, even if it is no longer Australian owned.

. . .

I've also brought my QUT (Queensland University of Technology) cap for the same purpose. It's a favourite cap because it's light and fits well. It might be useful if perhaps they support the stories from my journey and spread the word about my book.

So it's 1:20pm and I'm hungrily waiting for the in-flight meal to come. I retrieve the first half of the peanut butter and honey sandwich that my husband encouraged me to pack. I mock him relentlessly for travelling with sandwiches but today I was very grateful. As I'm eating my sandwich, the child on the other side of the plane woke up and starts wailing again. Groan. I put on my headphones and retrieve my magazines. After a few minutes the child settles. Oh the joy of a quiet cabin again. I read Time magazine and The Economist from cover to cover. Bliss. I'm never settled enough to do this at home. I've also got an ambitious list of books I'd like to read while I'm away. We'll see.

BUSTLING BANGKOK
25 JANUARY 2020

Krung Thep is the shortened name of the City of Angels that we more commonly know as Bangkok. The name is, well, rather beyond long, and it reminds me of the wonderful quirkiness of this city that was my home for five years from 2007 until 2012. Here's the full name if you're interested,

> *Krung Thep Mahanakhon Amon Rattanakosin Mahinthara Ayuthaya Mahadilok Phop Noppharat Ratchathani Burirom Udomratchaniwet Mahasathan Amon Piman Awatan Sathit Sakkathattiya Witsanukam Prasit*
> which means
> *The city of angels, the great city, the eternal jewel city, the impregnable city of God Indra, the grand capital of the world endowed with nine precious gems, the happy city, abounding in an enormous Royal Palace that resembles the heavenly abode where reigns the reincarnated god, a city given by Indra and built by Vishnukarma.*

Couldn't have said it better myself. If you ask a native Bangkokian where they live, be prepared for a long answer.

25 January 2020 – Arriving at Don Mueang Airport, Bangkok

Bangkok was my first port of call en route to Mae Sot in western Thailand, where the Soft Nut Bike Tour was to depart from.

My arrival into Don Mueang airport was memorable for the number of people wearing face masks. I was arriving as concerns about the spread of coronavirus were increasing exponentially. On arrival I'd forgotten how old and tatty the infrastructure is, belonging to a previous period. It's not all shiny and sparkly as is the newer Suvarnabhumi Airport. Although it's true that these days Don Mueang looks very old and small compared to Suvarnabhumi, for those who have been visiting Thailand for many years, it holds a lot of nostalgia. With its wooden decoration, there is a feeling upon arrival that you are somewhere special. Suvarnabhumi, with its glistening modernity could be an airport almost anywhere in the world.

I noticed that at least a third of all passengers were wearing masks. It's hard to tell I know most of the passengers were Asian and I'm not sure if these were from other Asian countries or from China, I figured I should really be wearing mine as well. If not to catch the coronavirus but just to stop getting any sort of cold or other virus that can easily be caught when you're crammed into tight spaces.

I groaned to myself when I noticed that we needed to be fingerprinted as we passed through immigration and we all used the same glass electronic scanning pad, read as petri dish, for getting our fingerprints done. If people have coronavirus they would easily be spread through this efficient process. I made a mental note to wash my hands as soon as possible.

I was pleased to see my bag was waiting for me and after a little bit of negotiation found my way through to Gate 5 - which was the agreed meeting point for the taxi. I saw my name written neatly in Thai and English on a piece of paper stuck on one of the metal grates separating arriving passengers from those greeting them. I looked around and there was no one there. I looked at a man on the other side of the fence, also waiting for someone else and shrugged my shoulders. He pointed over to a row of chairs near a wall and I could see a lady asleep. He called out to her, waking her from her slumbers and she came over rather sheepishly to say hello and take my bag. We had to walk some way to get to the car located at the end of the car park as the airport was busy.

It's always interesting walking through the airport and getting the sense of the sound and the activity. When you walk past bored girls on stools outside the massage parlours there's always the distinctive scent of Tiger Balm.

. . .

We finally emerged from the air-conditioned cocoon of the arrival's hall into the heat. It was sticky and unpleasant, and while a breeze was blowing, it did not in any way provide relief. I remember when I lived in Bangkok, missing the cool evening breeze.

The drive to the QC hotel on Soi 4 in the Nana district took longer than I expected. My driver chose motorways circling the city, exiting at Victory Monument and cutting through a creepy construction site that would have been ideal for any Jack Reacher novel. I made a mental note that even if the car broke down, I was definitely not going to get out.

We ended up on the road that runs past the Bumrungrad Hospital, which is well known for Arab restaurants, before we arrived at the entrance to Soi 4. It was a Saturday night and nearly impossible to enter because of traffic gridlock, although spicy food carts and purveyors of brooms were able to weave among the parked vehicles. After four changes of lights and some bold, pre-emptive moves, the taxi made it across and down Soi 4 without incident – which is always remarkable given the inebriated pedestrians and stray dogs on the road. The hotel was not obviously located at the GPS address so the taxi driver asked a street vendor who pointed down a narrow lane to the QC Guest House.

I was warmly greeted by two ladies with perfect English. I smiled and sighed. I'd arrived. I pulled my bag up two flights of stairs and was delighted that the Wi Fi worked, the bed was comfy and the sheets were crisp. There was no kettle but that was okay. I'd have to go out for my morning cup of tea. There was bottled water in the fridge and I made cold porridge which I consumed at 3am, five hours later, when I woke ready to start the day. Oh the bain of jet lag.

∽

Les' diary in Brisbane – 25 January 2020

Dropped Tracy at airport for her flight to BKK. Pleased I planned ahead and booked parking for $5 allowing me to have a last cup of coffee with her at the airport instead of just a fumbled farewell at kerbside.

Drove home stopping at DFO stores, ostensibly to look for a new frying pan as with Tracy away I'll be pushing my cooking skills to the limit. A myriad of choices proved too complicated for me to make the decision. Called in to the Merrel store and ended up buying three pairs of shoes for a total $127. Also checked out the underwear at Calvin Klein again it was all too complicated and I was so spoilt for choice I decided I didn't really need any new underwear. Forgot where the car was parked but found it eventually after wandering around for 20 minutes in the heat.

Quiet afternoon. Music and Netflix evening.

∽

Tracy's diary – 26 January 2020

Awake at six o'clock and again frequented nearby 7/11 to pick up coconut flavoured yogurts. It was deliciously cool and the street was spookily quiet. When I came downstairs later, I was delighted to be greeted by one of the receptionists saying, I looked beautiful. This was slightly bewildering, but it made me feel good.

After breakfast, I walked along the uneven pavement of Ruam Rudee Road down to All Seasons Place, which is a shopping and banking centre. I transferred funds to pay for my cycling trip which had not been possible from Australia. I then walked along Wireless Road, past the elegant US Ambassador's residence and up to Starbucks at Chit Lom, where I enjoyed a coffee and a familiar toasted crab sandwich while watching a troupe of street sweepers, gathering up rubbish while chatting amiably.

I then hopped on the BTS Sky train noting that 30% of people were wearing masks. It was sensible in such a crowded environment. However, it was tricky to wear a mask because my breathing constantly steamed up my glasses. I found myself constantly fiddling with it which I knew was unhygienic. I arrived at MBK (short for Mah Boon Krong) at National Stadium station, 30 minutes too early. Myself and 50 others sat on seats in the shade, socially distancing, while waiting for the shopping centre to open. Suddenly the security guards started energetically blowing their whistles, telling people to stop walking. It wasn't eight o'clock in the morning so it wasn't the daily broadcast of the national anthem to honour the King. Instead, a car with flashing lights came zipping along one of the crossroads to Sukhumvit transporting a member of the royal family.

Myriad of masks

It's been interesting observing the range of masks proliferating at market stalls. Mine is a fairly common mask which is clearly at the bottom end of the fashion spectrum. Other masks are styled in military camouflage or branded with logos such as 3M. Some black masks remind me of the apparatus worn by Hannibal Lecter in the film Silence of the Lambs. Positively frightening.

Massages and makeup

Getting a traditional Thai massage is one of the treats I miss most about not living here. I had a wonderful massage at MBK, and I felt like I could float outside. The masseur frequently pushed past that delicate pleasure / pain threshold with her bionic thumbs, but I didn't care.

After my massage I visited the stalls selling discounted makeup. I bought a lipstick and a lip pencil and was momentarily taken back when the vendor started dusting her wares with the 200 baht notes I'd given her. I'd forgotten that this is a normal Chinese practise for the first sale of the day, bringing good luck for the rest of the day's trading.

I came back to the hotel to discover that either the building had tipped or the person who tiled the bathroom floor had not engineered sufficient slope for the water to evacuate. Indeed, there were still two inches of water covering the bathroom floor. At this point I was pleased that my husband wasn't with me as he has a tendency to catch tinea and this little swimming pool was the perfect environment. The attentive staff came with mops and I made a mental note to have 30 second showers in future.

Les' diary – 26 January 2020

Walked to the market in Botanical Gardens slightly slower than usual due to my slowly recovering back. Pain au raisin from the French "boulanger" and coffee from the two friendly gay guys. Daydreamed about speaking French to the pastry guy, German to guy at Andy's German sausage and Thai to the lady at the Thai cafe. Did not do any of these things but practised alone on the way home.

Drove to my friend Andy's place for Australia Day BBQ. Tracy's absence required a sober visit as I had to drive myself both ways. So I was home by 5pm and took to the bottle then. More music and movies. Signed up for Amazon Prime so that I could watch the new Star Trek Picard show.

Unable to make it work on TV so saved most of the episode to watch in bed on my iPad.

Woken around midnight by noisy guests in apartment next door. Filled out online complaint form and issue fixed pretty quick. Couldn't get back to sleep so finished watching the latest episode of *Picard,* the latest incarnation of the Star Trek franchise. Excellent show and looking forward to the next episode.

Tracy - Monday 27th January 2020

On Monday morning, I caught the train to Saladeng. I was a little nervous about this trip to the Thai Social Security office even though I'd done it before with Les. I found the building and showed my form to staff at reception so they could direct me to the correct floor. I was fairly sure I needed to go to the second floor but I was sent to the third floor, where I was redirected back to the second floor. On arrival I observed that queuing system box, much like that exists in the supermarkets where you select the service you need by pressing the requisite button. All options were of course written in Thai. Luckily someone came out, looked at my form and pointed me to another room, but I was then redirected back to the lady who had originally helped me. Being passed around between people and rooms was the longest part of the process and I was processed within 10 minutes.

. . .

With my pension payment processed, I decided to walk back to the guest house through the lush green of Lumphini Park. At ten o'clock in the morning it wasn't crowded with just a few cyclists doing laps and various groups undertaking activities. For example, there were ladies dancing with fans and others engaged in Tai Chi. Monitor lizards and turtles languished on the grass in the shade.

I exited the park on Sarasin Road next to where we used to live although it was now unrecognisable with the removal of 1950s style barber nooks and crumbling eateries. I fondly remembered a Chinese restaurant where you used to be able to order *fish head in a deep pan* or *duck's blood*, although I never partook of these delicacies.

Les - Monday 27 January 2020

Walked in the park as usual. Extending the distance a bit each day and back slowly getting better. Wondered how Tracy was fairing with her trip to the Thai Social Security office but was confident she would be successful.

Tracy - Tuesday 28 January 2020

. . .

I've taken my first malaria tablet. Not as horrible as I remembered. I've got 28 to get through. Which reminds me that the bike trip is getting closer.

I've arranged to do a luggage swap with Chris. He's sending me a pannier we left at his place and he's taking my big suitcase which I will collect at journey's end. The taxi should arrive at 10:00. At 9:45 Chris calls to say taxi is running late. 10:30 call, *driver is stuck in traffic.* 11:15. *Driver is lost. Can I provide more instructions?* 11:30 Chris calls to say taxi driver has arrived. I say I can't see him and start waving my arms at all passing traffic. No luck. I ask Chris to get the taxi driver to call me and pass the phone to the local security guard – who provides further information in Thai. Bangkok is a difficult city to negotiate for locals and nearby impossible for *out of towners*. Anyway at 12:10 a taxi with an embarrassed driver arrives. He is smiling broadly which is disturbing as his teeth are stained red and I'm certain he's been in a major pileup on the freeway. My Thai is limited to food orders and giving instructions to drive more slowly so I'm unable to enquire as to what has happened. It will be several days until the source of "the accident" is revealed.

With images of the taxi driver's bloodied teeth embedded in my mind, I headed off to the dentist for a check-up and clean. This is always a highly professional experience with the dentist and her team donning protective head gear and using the latest equipment. With my teeth sorted I needed to catch a taxi back, which is easy at All Seasons as there are these immaculately dressed men wearing white military-styled suits and hats. Unfortunately, one of the valets was aggressively furrowing up his nose to remove something providing resistance. The contrasting images were stark. Picking your nose in public is not considered such a faux pas here as it is in other cultures.

Les – 28 January 2020

Began my back-stretching exercises as recommended by the physio. Painful but I could feel the benefit afterwards, much like a Thai massage. I reminisced about taking a stroll along the Soi to my favourite massage shop and enjoying a coffee or beer afterwards.

I also thought about my long held but never realised plan, to travel by train from Vietnam back to Bangkok. I'd intended to do this trip, and many like it, when I was living in Bangkok but people kept dying. I'd been in Bangkok for less than a year when I received the call that my mother had passed from a massive stroke. A few years later my father succumbed to his many ailments and he too left the world, dying peacefully in his sleep. It was only a year or two later that my elder brother, who had been unwell with an incorrectly diagnosed blood disorder, also departed this earth. This reminded me of the bike trips Ian, my brother, had accompanied me on when we lived in Thailand. He'd been with us when we explored the Laos side of the Mekong river which forms a natural border between the two countries. Never easy to please, he seemed to enjoy the journey, but take exception to the fact that garlic was a frequent additive, if not the main constituent, of most of the food dishes served at wayside cafés. The Lao and Thai languages are similar and I had a happy memory of learning the phrase *mai sai gratiem* (no garlic) to appease him. Unfortunately, a little like saying *no sugar,* this often seemed to be understood as *not too much.*

~

Tracy - Wednesday 29 January 2020

With my teeth cleaned and my pension sorted, I decided to reward myself with a day at my favourite Japanese spa, the Yunomori Onsen Spa at Khlong Toei. There are a myriad of pools and tubs of varying temperatures here to soothe the body and calm the mind. After an hour of soaking I was toasty-warm and limbered up and in preparation for another Thai massage.

I thought I'd been given a good deal when a tiny masseuse came out to reception to collect me. However, her looks were deceptive as she ignored my request for a *medium pressure* message which avoided my knee where an old ski injury has been making itself known as I'd been walking along the uneven streets of Bangkok. Her technique literally took my breath away and I was forced to push my fingernails into my palms to suppress my screams. Still, when it is over, my stress was relieved in addition to the skin on my hands.

. . .

I tipped my torturer nonetheless, and went outside to hail a taxi. There were numerous motorcycle taxis around which are fast, efficient and occasionally fatal. I had promised Les that I would only take taxi cabs so walked down to the nearest crossroad and managed to pull over an elderly gentleman who wasn't perplexed by the idea of transporting a farang female. (Farang is a term Thais use to describe Europeans). I asked to go to Soi 31, which means Soi Sukhumvit 31 in 99% of cases– except in this case.

I was driven into unknown but interesting areas of Bangkok I'd never visited before. After twenty minutes my elderly driver stopped at a petrol station to ask directions and finally pulled into a Soi 31 somewhere miles away on the other side of town. I indicated that this was not Soi 31 Sukhumvit so he said the magic words of BTS and dropped me at Surasek BTS station which is probably about 10 kilometres from my intended destination. From here I was able to navigate my way back to Asok via a change at Siam station. As I made my way out from the Sky train I spotted a rodent I'd seen the day before. This rat was distinctive because he was obese and walked slowly. And that's the first thing you notice because most rats don't walk slowly. This one also had grey and white stripes and was clearly accustomed to multiple people passing. He seemed to have a home under a concrete slab beside the food vendors carts; a *rat heaven* of sorts. I looked at him – he looked at me, and we both scuttled off to the place where we would lay our heads for the night.

. . .

I pay attention to rats; they're both bolshy and intelligent. Watching this rat reminded me of an incident in Bangkok thirty years previously when Les and I were passing through during a late breaking monsoon. The streets were mini canals and everyone was looking for higher ground. We braved the downpour and sat at a table in a deserted restaurant. Well we thought it was deserted. Movement caught our eye and we noticed three rats sitting on the table next to ours. The waitress came to take our order and we pointed to the rodents. She giggled, and pointed the rats out to her colleagues behind the counter. She returned her attention to us, held the pen above her notepad and waited for us to order. Les and I glanced at each other and decided we weren't hungry anymore.

Les – Wednesday 29 January 2020

I decided today was the day I would up my recovery regime and went for a short bike ride. Fortunately, nobody saw me struggle to mount my bike in the solitude of the building's garage. I grimaced slightly as I lifted my leg over the back wheel but once in the saddle the pain was only minimal.

I rode a couple of kilometres along by the Brisbane river and began to convince myself that maybe I could still board a flight to Bangkok and join the others on the trip. This foolhardy dream subsided when I stopped for a drink and found that getting off the bike was actually harder and more painful than getting on had been. Obviously my recuperation still had a long way to go.

Tracy - Thursday 30 January 2020

Departure day arrived and I was worrying that my panniers would be too heavy. Air Asia has strict weight requirements for luggage carried onboard. Worst case scenario, I'd pay excess baggage on the plane and have to pedal harder on the road. On the positive side, if my bags were heavier, I'd lose more weight. The taxi wasn't coming for a couple of hours. Hanging around is always hard so I turned the TV on to CNN and watched senators asking Donald Trump's lawyers questions about his impeachment. I was nervous and excited at this wonderful and easy opportunity to remove him from office. But would they? I couldn't believe the number of times I was thinking, surely this time he's got to go.

While waiting for the taxi I receive a note from Chris telling me that I didn't need to pick up my bike from the bus station next to Mae Sot airport as previously arranged. My bike buddies Jeannine, Jean and David had gone through the tortuous process of collecting everyone's bikes the day before. Apparently, the administration process had taken several hours and was followed by a precarious ride on a narrow main road without a safe verge and with large thundering vehicles sweeping past. I was relieved and disappointed in equal measure. Relieved because I was acutely aware of the limitations of my Thai and knew the bike retrieval was unlikely to be straightforward. Disappointed because this was a curious challenge at the beginning of the Burmese adventure.

I arrived at Don Mueang early to discover that my plane had been delayed by an hour. I spent the time sorting through my luggage identifying anything else that was discardable. Air Asia had signs prominently displayed saying two bags only were allowed on board – that were not to be heavier than seven kilos together. I made the decision to aggressively sort through my luggage on arrival in Mae Sot and then head to the post office to send unnecessary items back to Hidden Holiday House (HHH), which was the final stop on the tour. Packing is always a challenge and I take great pride in the thought I put into the process. On this occasion, I'd been tardy. My packing list is provided below.

Essential cycling packing

- Tin cup and spoon
- Twinning's Lady Grey Earl Grey tea
- Uncle Toby's Brown Sugar and Cinnamon instant porridge
- Lawrence of Arabia hat with flaps
- Removable sleeves
- Laundry washing bag (Wash cycling gear every day, and if not dry put in laundry bag on back of bike)
- 2 bike pants and 2 bike shirts on rotation.
- Sarong come makeshift sheet. Can be dressed up

for evening wear when needed. Can also be converted to additional pillow if needed, by wrapping up clothes
- Clothes washing liquid
- Super strong zinc
- Suntan cream
- Knee braces
- Small sweat towels – Boy you need these
- Underwear

Prior to departure from Brisbane my sister said she thought it interesting that I was taking instant porridge to avoid constipation. She had clearly never been on a ten-day biking tour before.

~

Les – 30 January 2020

I met my friend Michael for coffee today. We'd become friends in Bangkok where we had met at a pub quiz. We'd stayed in touch and both returned to Brisbane at roughly the same time. He was sympathetic to my plight as he also wanted to travel but was somewhat restricted by his responsibility of looking after ageing parents.

He's about the same age as me and we consoled each other and discussed our various ailments; my back and high cholesterol, his walking issues due to gout along with high blood pressure. Anyone listening in would have gone away thinking we were a sorry pair.

Tracy – A few snaps from Bangkok follow

Waiting for MBK shopping centre to open

Mask shopping

Bustling Bangkok

One of many massages

Lottery ticket seller

Picking up fresh juice from street vendors

Sukhumvit Road, Bangkok

Lumphini Park Bangkok

Tortoises sunning themselves in Lumphini Park

PART II

SOFT NUT BIKE TOUR OF BURMA

Mae Sot. I know it's down there somewhere

BORDER TOWN - MAE SOT
30 JANUARY 2020

The countryside looked crispy-dry as my delayed Nok Air flight sliced through the hazy clouds to land at Mae Sot. I was amused to see the words International Airport above the hangar-like building as we walked across the tarmac and was impressed they checked my temperature. There was no queue for taxis and once I'd confirmed that the ride into town was only going to cost me one hundred baht, I relaxed.

I was delighted by the warm welcome I received at J2 Hotel. I was the only one staying here from my tour as the T Guest House where my cycling buddies were staying, was booked out. I tipped the contents of my panniers on to the bed and created two piles; one for nice-to-have, the other, essentials. I shoved the non-essential clothes into a plastic sack and set off to find the post office.

Mae Sot was one of those towns where vehicles park on the pavement in front of the shops and you're forced to walk on the road. I avoided becoming a statistic and soon stumbled upon a rather lovely café and decided to get a drink and see if I could get directions to the post office.

I noted that there were a few well-dressed Europeans with laptops open inside. A sure sign the beverages were good. While there are many Europeans working in Bangkok, they seemed out of place here in Mae Sot. I speculated, but didn't confirm, that they were working for the UN or a similar NGO. I asked them if they were local and knew where the post office was. They indicated that they lived and working in Myanmar and had just come over for the day. I wondered if they had crossed the border just to drink the coffee. I queried their sanity the following evening after I had experienced the road from Myawaddi to Hpa An, and concluded that they must have been truly desperate for a quality beverage.

After I'd ordered my banana smoothie, I asked for directions to the post office with my limited Thai. A map was drawn and hand signals made indicating the direction I needed to take. The post office was only one kilometre away. Staff at the post office were smiley and helpful and I was relieved when my excess clothing was on its way to HHH.

With the jobs for the day done, I was free to explore Mae Sot. I stopped to admire the amulets that a tuk tuk driver was selling while waiting for customers. I enjoying looking at the food markets and magnificent fabric swatches on display in shop windows. Now I'd cleared a bit of room in my panniers, surely there was going to be space for a few pieces of fabric? The style of traditional clothes in the windows were more Burmese than Thai, which was not surprising given that I later learnt from an uncited source on Wikipedia, that nearly 200,000 folk from Myanmar live in Mae Sot.

I bumped into my cycling friends while touring the town and followed them to their guest house to collect my bike. My bike was rather dirty having been resting outside in Chris's shed for twelve months so I treated her to a personal spa treatment at a garage across the road from my hotel. For the princely sum of $1.50, four young men made my bike sparkle. Twenty four hours later I wondered why I had bothered. Still, like the rest of us, we like to start any journey looking and feeling refreshed.

Les – 30 January 2020

I lay in bed aware that today was the day Tracy and I had been scheduled to fly from Bangkok to the border town of Mae Sot. When I'd booked the flights for the two of us I'd had slightly mixed feelings of trepidation and excitement. Nok Air, the local airline who operate the route, use small propeller driven aircraft and whilst on a sunny windless day these afford a wonderful view of the countryside due to their low flightpath, throw in some bad weather, a thunderstorm perhaps or high winds and it becomes something of a roller coaster ride.

. . .

I remembered our experiences years before flying from Sydney to the small regional airport of Belmont, close to where Tracy's parents were living. Beautiful views of Sydney Harbour and the coast for the most part but on our last trip the weather was bad and the 25 minute trip seemed like a lifetime, one that was about to end.

I was also sorry not to be reuniting with our cycling friends from previous trips.

CROSSING THE FRONTIER
31 JANUARY 2020

We were all excited as we gathered together at the T guest house the following morning. Departure day had arrived. My French friends were still having breakfast, snacking on tamarind fruit grown by the owner. It wasn't to my liking, so I politely declined a second round.

Chris our fearless leader, and his wife Areeya, had arrived into Mae Sot that morning after an overnight bus trip. There's no way I could do this. Chris was as fresh as ever, checking that we were all fine and that our tyres were pumped and ready to go. Areeya was keen to show us the beautiful new panniers that she had insisted Chris buy for 'his birthday'. She had commented on how once the bike tools were loaded into the old panniers how little room remained for even one day's worth of clothing. They would be riding a tandem with their magnificent new panniers, a proud Thai flag and a huge plastic crate. Saying they were riding the tandem is probably a little generous as Areeya's contribution was, well...how shall I put this. She spent 90% of her time taking photos, wonderful photos from her back seat vantage point on the bike, and every now and then, remembering to pedal. She also did a stellar job of buying snacks en route that were kept in the plastic crate for our consumption.

It was an easy 8 kilometre ride to the border. Easy only in the sense that it was a nice sealed road. I like sealed roads. This was the main highway into Myanmar and a myriad of trucks pummelled along the busy road. I felt like we were the ibis birds among the hippos, weaving in and out among these dangerous, slow moving beasts.

Everyone, except Thai nationals needed a tourist visa. Or so we thought. As is often the way with visa rules, rules change. While it was perfectly fine for Thai nationals to fly into Myanmar and get a visa on arrival, the same rules did not apply to land crossings. For a short while it looked like two of our party would be going home.

While Chris stayed behind with Areeya and Teerayud, the rest of us continued with the processing, which involved providing the same information on different forms in different rooms and then handing over our electronically generated visas, which surely had captured all the information they had just asked of us twice. It's a pity you're not allowed to take photos at immigration processing points as I felt like I'd been transported back to my second-grade classroom with consideration for the age of the desks and the quality of the pencils. One clear exception was the supervisor who wore a most magnificent longyi and satin top, a look you'd expect to see on the stage of an Italian opera and not on a bridge, connecting two countries.

The Moei River demarcates the border between Thailand and Myanmar in this area. There was an important midpoint on the bridge over the Moei River where you cross the chasm – metaphorically speaking, between two countries and two sets of rules. Thai immigration was on one side of the bridge, and the Myanmar processing centre at the other end. Once most of us were processed, Chris advised us to ride into town and exchange money and buy sim cards. I've often found it overwhelming to arrive in a new country by land, and certainly arriving on a bicycle is a special experience.

When we reached the middle of the bridge between Thailand and Myanmar, we swapped from the left to right hand side of the road, moving quickly to avoid the oncoming traffic. In Myanmar they used to drive on the left-hand side of the road. The switch came on December six, 1970 after General U Ne Win observed that most nations drive on the right and proposed that Myanmar follow suit because the country would have to connect to international road networks in the future. It was rumoured at the time that U Ne Win took the step on the advice of an astrologer, in order to avert impending bad luck. Many people believed that General U Ne Win misinterpreted the astrologer's words, which purportedly were meant to persuade him to abandon socialism and reintroduce a market economy.

What is curious or rather inconvenient about the side of the road used is that Myanmar imports its cars second-hand from left-hand driving Thailand and Japan. Drivers therefore have to rely on a passenger to give them the all-clear for overtaking, or simply good luck.

Chaos abounded as we dismounted our bikes. There were people everywhere on the main road and heavily loaded cars passed narrowly by, honking their horns. Even more concerning, was that we had clearly arrived not long after a major traffic accident as there was blood and bits of flesh scattered everywhere on the road. It felt akin to arriving on the set of Mad Max. We found a space to gather with our bikes in relative safety while half the troupe left to change money. Our bikes attracted a lot of attention, with some locals asking in English how much the bikes cost. I was embarrassed by the question and kept replying 'don't know very old' which was true as my Decathlon beauty had been purchased in 1997, but still our possessions showed that we had money. The conversation was interrupted by a dreadful guttural sound and I turned to see a man spit a crimson projectile on to the road. On closer observation I observed that his lips were stained red. A light bulb went off and I smiled. There'd not been an accident after all. The bloody parts on the road were the chewy remains of betel nut which is a hallucinogenic snack favoured by the local population. We were to see the smashed-like-cherry remains on many footpaths throughout the tour and clearly the taxi driver in Bangkok who I thought had been in an accident had also been partaking of this treat.

Once the rest of the crew made it through immigration our bikes and panniers were loaded onto a small pick-up truck and we piled into a minivan, excited to escape the chaos and continue to our first town of Hpa An. I was looking forward to the journey and to seeing some of the countryside. We were entering via the Kayin (Karen) state of Myanmar. There are 135 ethnic identities in Myanmar which are grouped into eight major ethnic races including Bamar, Chin, Kachin, Kayin, Kayah, Mon, Rakhine and Shan.

Chris had told us that the 140 kilometre journey to Hpa An (pronounced Pa An) would take four hours. This didn't make sense, particularly when we cruised along forty kilometres of the beautiful bitumen *friendship road* that the Thai government had built from Myawaddi, inland. And then the bitumen stopped and the *bumpity bump* began. Not only was the ride extremely unpleasant, but the traffic was kicking up the dust covering all trees and plant life with a dull browny-red facade. How little I had appreciated the diversity of colours we enjoyed until I had so few to see for hours on end. We passed several Karen checkpoints, reminding us which state we were in. We continued to trundle along with many other trucks, utes and mini vans. This trip will be remembered as one of the most boring parts of the tour.

Our lunch stop was a Thai restaurant in a small village called Ein Du. We all felt a little guilty to be eating Thai and not Burmese food but we needed a little reward after the harrowing journey so far. While our food was being prepared I stood on the edge of the street to take in my surroundings. An elegant lady rode by on her bike carrying an umbrella to keep the sun off. She was wearing a lovely htamein (sarong), long sleeved white cotton top and thongs – not my preferred choice for cycling. It didn't take me long to realise that all the women wear sarongs when cycling. Indeed, they wear sarongs all the time, even if they are breaking rocks at the side of the road. Men tended to wear longyis, which is a piece of fabric wrapped around and knotted at the front, in addition to sarongs and more western-like trousers. I loved looking at advertising posters which demonstrated the prevalence of traditional clothing with European fashions, having some influence among the young.

Ten kilometres out from Hpa Ana, a majestic limestone outcrop appeared known as Zwegabin. The Karen people consider this mountain sacred and it has become the state's symbol. Hpa An was bustling with activity and our hotel was right in the centre. I'd been looking forward to arriving after the long day's journey. With the name of Golden Palace Hotel, there had been an expectation that the night's accommodation would be something grand. My room wasn't ready so I went up on to the roof to view my surrounds. I could see the beautiful Zwegabin mountain range in the distance, perfectly framed for a photo between two tall palm trees. There were excitable roosters out the back, tuk tuks out the front and a mosque next door.

We all met downstairs to check that our bikes were ok after the bumpy journey from the border and set off for a local tour. The town sat on the river Thanlwin (Salween). The river's edge was not beautiful but there was beauty in watching the long boats chugging up and down the river. We noticed a large tourist boat and discovered there was a tour departing shortly. With beverages purchased and arrangements made for our bikes to be minded, we took our seats on the upper deck. I'm in danger of waxing lyrically here as it turned out to be a fabulous cruise. Not only did we get multiple opportunities to take calendar quality photos as the sun set, mingle with other mostly Burmese tourists, but we stopped outside a rocky plinth where eagles were soaring, and watched thousands of bats depart their cave, creating a huge ribbon-like pattern in the sky as they moved en-mass in search of food. The eagles had the same idea and were diving into the throng snagging their evening meal. It was easy pickings.

We returned to the jetty and walked to a nearby night market where there was a wonderful smorgasbord of food choices on offer. I passed on the deep-fried crickets, choosing samosas, spicy Thai chicken dish and an avocado smoothie. There was a great feel to the market and I enjoyed observing families with small children and grandparents eating together around tiny tables.

Les – 31 January 2020

Border crossing day for the cycling team so I celebrate by having some packet Phad Thai from Woolies. I discovered it was Phad Thai in name only, a poor substitute for the delicious meals I knew my friends were having. I consoled myself with a fine Portugese red wine which I knew was unlikely to be available in a small Thai town

Continuing with physio visits at the hospital outpatients which break up the monotony a bit. In fact I am seeing two physiotherapists. One at the hospital where I was admitted on the day of my injury and another supplied by the doctor I saw later – an interesting feature and convenient glitch, of the Australian medical system. The two worked in very different ways.

At the hospital there was very little physical contact, which seemed odd as I was having physiotherapy. Martin, the young man who had been assigned to me would gently suggest various exercises and quietly watch a I did them, all the while whispering encouragement.

At the doctors it was all about contact. I'd lie on the bed with my face in a hole looking at the floor while my nemesis pushed and prodded at the tight muscles in my back. Elbows were frequently used and this again reminded me of the first few Thai massages I'd had, before I leant to say *mai aow* and *mai chawp* (*don't want, don't like*).

MAJESTIC MOUNTAINS - HPA AN
1 FEBRUARY 2020

I was woken the following morning at 5:45 by music calling people to prayers. I rolled out of bed and put the kettle on and blew the circuit in the room. So, no tea and no warm shower.

One of our troupe, (Tseng) was turning 50 today but could not join us as he needed to stay in bed to celebrate, having eaten something dodgy from the night market the day before.

Departure time was 6:30am which is important, because even though we were undertaking the bike tour during the 'cool season', it becomes unbearably hot from ten until four each day. The ride out of town was slightly hazardous because of local driving styles and very interesting because of the varying architecture. Lots of old timber buildings. We rode past pagodas and skirted rice fields. There were many beautiful vantage points with the Zwegabin mountain as a backdrop. Our troupe was a curiosity and we were warmly greeted with Minglaba (hello) by locals as we rode by. I had a man on a motorbike ride beside me for some distance.

'Where you going?' he asked.
  'Don't know,' I replied honestly. I had difficulty remembering the names of towns and temples but began priming myself to answer this question as it was often asked along with,
  'Where you name' and 'I love you'.

The first stop of the day was at Kyauk Kalat pagoda which was ten kilometres out of Hpa-An. It's a working monastery, but shoe-free visitors are allowed. The pagoda sat somewhat perilously I thought, on the top of a narrow limestone pinnacle on a small island in the middle of a lake. It made for an impressive photo.

I realised upon arrival that I had forgotten to bring my sarong which is required to provide modesty by covering my knees for entry into all temples. Luckily, there were clothing markets at the temple, as there often are, and I purchased a beautiful pink, purple, blue and silver striped scarf – which would take up only a little room in my pannier. There were children squealing with delight playing tag while their parents made sticky rice which they were keen to share with us.

We had to remove our shoes to visit the island on which the pagoda sat. I understand the need for cleanliness indoors but when you are walking outside the no-shoes rule irritates me.

A red cotton string was tied around our wrist as we entered the base of the pagoda. I then attempted to climb to the top, but the first steps had been recently washed and were incredibly slippery, presenting a HUGE occupational health and safety hazard. I retreated and returned to the edge of the island to re-shoe. I was more than a little irritated to observe two monks walking past in flip-flops while I tied up my laces. I hate the different rules for locals versus visitors and I HATE having dirty feet.

An hour later we were on the road again, passing thatched cottages and small trucks overloaded with hay. We were fortunate to stumble upon the celebration of the opening of a pagoda. Hundreds of people were decked out in colourful costumes. We dispersed into the crowd to soak in the carnival atmosphere. A while later Chris tried to round us up but was having difficulty extracting Jean and Jeannine from a tent where they were taking tea and pastries with the Burmese military!

With a little bit of coaxing we were all soon back on our bikes. I pause at this moment to reflect on road surfaces. We started the day cruising on concrete or bitumen. Heaven for cycling. We were of course on relatively main roads, which Chris likes to avoid wherever possible. It did not take long after departing the celebrations at the pagoda, for Chris to pull us over and advise us all to don our face masks as we were about to change road surfaces again. Indeed, we turned onto a deserted, but dusty track. As was the case on the road to Hpa-An, plant foliage was covered in boring browny-red dirt, making the scenery boring but providing relatively smooth riding. Sprinkled along the route, it was great to discover earthen pots filled with water sitting in shady spots. They had been placed there for the benefit of travellers by local people, who as Buddhists, hoped to get merit from these thoughtful actions. We were certainly very grateful.

Arrival onto a concrete road was the first sign we were approaching an area of higher road traffic. Large buses powering past were the second sign that a tourist destination was looming. The mountain which contains the Sadder Cave majestically rose up before us. As always, there were markets at the entrance to the cave selling refreshments and clothes. Being a religious place, we were required to remove our shoes. I kind of didn't mind this too much at temples and pagodas but for a large cave, where I could hear the distinctive screeching of bats, who were clearly dropping poop on the floor, I was irritated. My irritation increased when we visited the first Buddha who was reclining under carnival-like flashing lights. Chris had joked that this icon was colloquially called the 'disco Buddha'. The cave was impressive, although the reclining Buddha was tacky and I was grateful I made it out the other side without stubbing a toe.

At the entrance to the far side of the cave there was a vendor selling tortoises and fish that people could buy to release into the nearby river to make merit. I was most keen to buy a bottle of water and sat down on a bench with my hand sanitiser and scrubbed my feet as best I could before pulling on my socks and shoes again. Not being so enamoured with either caves or disco Buddhas, I was one of the first from our tour to make it out to the other side. I watched a group of young men practice their boxing skills with enthusiasm under a tree, while a woman walked past with two pigs at her heels. There was music with a distinctive Indian influence blaring out from a portable music box sitting high in a tree. When my fellow cyclists emerged, Chris informed us that there was an opportunity to visit Hai Shin cave a short distance away.

'But I've just cleaned my feet,' I puffed. 'I'm happy to wait outside and mind everybody's shoes.'

And indeed I sat on a rock and watched the pigs eat while the roosters scratched the dry earth. I'd chosen a lovely place to sit and survey a green field surrounded by the dramatic limestone cliffs.

When the others emerged from Hai Shin cave, we walked down to the river's edge and caught long tail boats back to the front of the cave where we'd parked our bikes. We were soon back on dirt roads heading to the Kaw Kathaoung cave on the east side of Zwegabin. It was not as picturesque as Saddar Cave, but is a sacred place for the locals due to the Buddha relic enshrined inside. It was next to a large swimming hole surrounded by many restaurants. The swimming hole was being enjoyed by many children. I felt a little sorry for the girls swimming in their long sarongs, but they seemed not to be encumbered by the wet fabric. I don't remember what we ate for lunch, but it was delicious, probably because it was two o'clock and served with local Karen wine.

After visiting the cave and the maze out front we enjoyed a straightforward ride back into Hpa An after lunch on a bitumen road shared with overloaded trucks. On arrival at the Golden Palace I checked to see if the electricity had been restored to my room.

'Oops I forgot' came the shy reply.

We enjoyed a Burmese feast for dinner at the San Ma Tau restaurant at a cost of $2 each. To top off a nice meal I was delighted to discover that the electricity to my room had been restored by the time we returned.

Les – 1 February 2020

I'm a bit surprised not to have any news from Tracy. I later find out that although she bought a SIM card for her phone at the Thai/Myanmar border she didn't insert it properly in the phone so she is incommunicado for a day or two. I'm reminded of the general ease of communication these days compared to when I started travelling and the best you could hope for was a letter waiting at the next Poste Restante.

HPA AN TO MAWLAMYINE
2 FEBRUARY 2020

Today's ride was estimated to be sixty four kilometres. Three of our troupe decided to take a boat to Mawalamyine rather than ride this distance in the heat. [It's worth giving some demographics about our group here. Our average age was 60 and with a range from 49 to 71.]

Our smaller group departed early Sunday morning, riding on sandy tracks along the Salween river. It was very picturesque. We passed small villages with thatched roof huts where locals were sometimes butchering animals. Chris kept joking that this was the appointed breakfast stop. We began to see the first of many signs featuring a photo of Aung San Su Kyi, with the message, 'We stand with you.' We stopped for breakfast at a small restaurant at the foot of the Kawgoon cave, which had also been converted into a religious complex. It was popular with locals as evidenced by the arrival of multiple trucks. We were somewhat of a curiosity now we'd left the big town of Hpa An as there were few foreigners around.

Kawgoon Cave and temple is both dramatic and beautiful. The cave has a rich history having said to have been worshipped by a Mon Queen in the 7th century. Since then sculptures and buildings have been added and replaced many times. The walls and ceilings are covered by thousands of small painted stucco images of Buddha. There were flocks of birds circling the temple enhancing the dramatic feel of the location.

I wore a favourite red batik sarong over my bicycle pants into the temple attracting the attention of a few shy girls who wanted to have their photo taken with me. I even had a family send their reluctant daughter over for a selfie-snap. Delighted with the result they then sent over their son who was even more reluctant. And then the mother came back, with the father and children straggling behind and I was featured in a family photo. I smile when I think about this portrait hanging on someone's wall.

Leaving behind my fans, we cycled again through the countryside. They were narrow dirt paths, lumbering along but highly rideable with only the occasional sand bog. We stopped to play with puppies and chat to a farmer in a field growing beans before taking dirt roads with pre-war looking vehicles. Many had been reconfigured in the most unusual way, highlighting the farmers' ingenuity. All villages had small stores where we could buy drinks and snacks like nuts or ice cream and there were also enterprising folk who set up cooking platforms off their motor scooters. We enjoyed deep fried spring rolls and samosas with chilli sauce.

We needed to cross the Salween River which forms the border between the Kayin and Mon states. We arrived at our transportation, which was a floating raft-like platform of six by six metres, suspended on oil drums with four propellers stuck out the back, and a child of about seven managing the rope tying at both ends of the journey. I took a space on the raft next to a lady with a full face of Thanaka makeup and a well-behaved chicken clutched to her chest. The white and yellowish makeup is worn extensively by women and children, with younger girls experimenting with designs.

The mercury was now rising steeply. This made it hard to take in all that was around me. I put my head down and concentrated hard to ride through the repressive heat. Chris never seemed to be affected by something as minor as 98% humidity, pointing out items of interest and frequently stopping to chat with locals. I can remember riding up one particularly dusty track in the middle of the day when the sun was at its most vicious. Chris got us to stop to discuss the differences between Thai and Burmese spirit houses. I love to learn about different cultures but when my basic needs for survival were not being addressed, I had difficulty being enthusiastic. Indeed, I may have even resorted to sarcasm. I was embarrassed by my behaviour, so when Chris next stopped and asked, who would like to climb 150 steps to a viewpoint of all the pagodas, I agreed. (Well I didn't have to take off my shoes and socks). The others remained at the bottom of the hill to *mind the bikes*, an activity that was highly unnecessary but always popular.

Despite my frequent and liberal application of sun cream at every stop, I was getting sunburnt. I was worried about getting prickly heat rash on my legs which I'd acquired on previous trips as it's a bothersome condition. By and large

I'd enjoyed the riding and knew that with 45 kilometres already covered there was only 19 to go.

We were now back on a smooth bitumen road, largely on our own, except for the occasional piece of farm equipment or a motor scooter transporting one to five people, smiling broadly as they passed. It goes without saying that no one was wearing a helmet. The last stretch of road before lunch was very exposed. It was very smooth and we were travelling fast but it was unprotected and hot. My attention was focused on just getting finished.

As is often the way, at the moment when we all were ready for lunch, there was nowhere to eat. We stopped at a house to buy water and asked if she prepared meals. She said no. Areeya noticed that she sold packet noodles, had sprouts in her kitchen and chickens running around the yard – all of which are ingredients for Kway Teow, one of our staple meals on the road. Chris explained that she didn't realise we had low standards and were very hungry.

The lunch stop was on a busy road, popular with large trucks honking frequently to warn of their impending arrival. I was horrified seeing the small children of the woman cooking lunch, riding their bikes on this busy thoroughfare.

Sated after lunch, we were all in good humour, particularly as we only had 19 kilometres to go by road and a short trip by boat. We continued on narrow concrete paths with a steep drop on either side along by the river. There was only room for one bike on the path, so there was frequent dismounting required when we faced motorcycles who used these paths as main thoroughfares. It was low tide on arrival and there was a path made of rocks through the mud to the long-tail boats waiting to transport us to Malwalamyine.

Our bikes and panniers were stacked up one end and we all squashed into the other. Two boats were required to transport the seven of us. I sighed as I sat down in a pool of water and mud. We putted along for a bit and then pulled up to an island called Shampoo Island. This small island has a spring used to supply water for royal hair-washing ceremonies and has a couple of religious building and sculptures. Areeya, jumped ashore and was immediately scolded by the boat operator for wearing her shoes on hallowed land. I groaned audibly. 'I'm staying in the boat,' I cried out which was echoed by other troupe members. Areeya hopped back in the boat and we abandoned Shampoo Island and headed towards Malwalamyine, which was now no more than 200 metres away.

Mawlamyine used to be called Moulmein and was the British capital of lower Burma. It is now the capital of the Mon state and the fourth largest city in Myanmar. The city is divided into two separate areas by a small mountain range topped with impressive pagodas. Malwalamyine is also famous because it was where George Orwell, author of Burmese Days, was stationed from 1922 until 1927.

The Than Lwin Seesar Hotel was in the old town looking out over the Gulf of Martaban. There was an enormous, bright yellow generator out front, providing early warning of potential power outages. Our French compatriots travelling here by boat, had not yet arrived. I joined Chris and Areeya in taking a tour of the town. While the main markets were closed there were smaller fish and chicken markets attracting trade. There were many crumbling colonial- style buildings, interspersed with brightly painted tea houses. Gorgeous images of folk dressed up in traditional costumes drinking tea were flying high on advertising banners. We headed up towards the colonial era prison. This was obviously Chris' suggestion. It wasn't immediately clear if the prison was still in operation. Certainly no one stopped Chris from entering through the arch way leading to the first layer of this complex. Areeya and I nervously followed. There were people living in small buildings inside the first wall as were a number of scabby dogs. We were ignored by both parties and I was delighted when we exited on the other side.

I returned to the hotel to wait for our compatriots arriving by boat while Chris and Areeya went off in search of other potentially dangerous areas to explore. Challenges in travelling in a group are familiar to many. It only takes one person to be late, annoying, or with impossible to meet dietary requirements, to fracture group cohesion. We were actually a pretty convivial troupe although we did have our communication challenges – and not just because of the multiple languages spoken. Miscommunication or lack of communication was easy to achieve. Helpfully, Chris had created a Soft Nut Group on Messenger, where morning start times were reported and curious sites about town noted. We were lucky that everywhere we stayed had internet connection, even if it meant precariously leaning over the balcony to get a signal. Unfortunately, not everyone had purchased a local SIM card so were reliant on these connections for keeping in touch.

Our first miscommunication came Sunday evening. Chris called me to report that a few of our troupe had found a nice vantage point on the pier for enjoying pre-dinner drinks while watching the sunset. Could I share the arrangement with the French troupe, who were staying on my floor, as he couldn't call them. I tapped on the door.

'*Oui*'

I could hear the shower running and guessed that they had only just arrived.

'Chris says we are meeting on the pier for pre-dinner drinks.'

'*Ce n'est pas possible*' *(it's not possible)* came the cranky response.

Silence.

'*D'accord*', (OK) I replied and then left to collect my bike to join my compatriots.

Chris asked if I had communicated the evening plans. I confirmed I had and reported the '*Ce n'est pas possible*' response and he then sent a message to let them know where we were.

We pulled together two tables in front of a stall specialising in southern Indian food and ordered avocado shakes, soaking in the local ambiance. The calm was soon disturbed by the arrival of our fiery French friends – who had felt abandoned. Tempers flared and then settled. The French troupe hadn't obtained the wi-fi password so hadn't seen the message about our location. You can see how communication challenges can create the proverbial storm in a tea cup.

Les – 2 February 2020

I check the itinerary and note with a fair amount of *Schadenfreude* that today is one of the longest cycling days of the trip at 64 kms. Not so far you might say. But remember it's going to be hot, dusty and humid. The "road" will in all likelihood be a series of bumps held together by potholes and no matter how much water you drink you're going to sweat twice as much out.

I strolled into town for a coffee and enjoyed another Brisbane summer's day which was a pleasant 28 degrees with a cooling breeze. No motorbikes, no trucks and no dust.

MAWLAMYINE
3 FEBRUARY 2020

Monday was technically a rest day. Well it may have been a rest day from riding, but not from sightseeing. We squeezed into a truck/tuk-tuk/tractor contraption with two narrow planks on either side on which to place our bottoms.

Our driver Arman, used to be a teacher and had lived in Mae Sot in Thailand for eight years. He joked that Mae Sot comprised 100,000 people from Myanmar and 14 from Thailand. We visited a small hut in the village of Dudong, where a man made small chalkboards for every student in the country. Not sure how long it will be until his expertise is no longer needed.

We then visited an equally quaint rubber band production factory, with the term *factory* being a little generous. The same could be said for the shirtless man sitting cross legged on the floor wrapping tobacco by hand called Cheroot or the young girl making hats from bamboo leaves. We stopped at a market store to buy longis for the boys in advance of a visit to a temple requiring them. There were also sarongs made of magical colours and to this day, I regret not purchasing a gorgeous swathe of fabric in light grey and dusty pink. A visit to the Bilu island revealed villagers making tobacco pipes and walking sticks. I felt sorry for the traders as none of us were very interested in buying trinkets which would be problematic to transport. My embarrassment was compounded by their generosity in giving us chilled bottled water.

We then all piled back into the truck to head off to the next location which was (another) reclining Buddha. It's hard work being a tourist sometimes; all that squeezing into a tiny truck, bouncing and jolting along a dusty potholed track only to be disgorged at yet another "must see" location. There were gentle grumbles beginning to bubble with calls for a refreshment break as a priority.

We arrived at the big reclining Buddha an hour later and Chris announced that there was to be an iced coffee break *after* the visit. Manu could take no more and suddenly announced,

'*Non Non Non*. Mutiny. We strike. *Liberté, égalité, fraternité*'. (He didn't actually say this, but I'm sure he wanted to). It was in that moment that the Soft Nut Bike Tour Union was formed. 'Come, we discuss terms over iced coffee.'

Chris shrugged his shoulders, everyone laughed and followed Manu over to a small stand where refreshing beverages were purchased. With everyone refreshed, Chris tried to rally enthusiasm with the promise that this Buddha was very impressive.

'Do I have to take my shoes off again Chris?'

'Tracy, you know the answer to that question'. I sighed. It wasn't just the prospect of another Buddha which was driving my intransigence. I needed alone time, as my morning porridge was not effectively countering the impact of hours spent in the saddle, or squashed up in the back of a tiny truck. The local bathroom facilities at the big reclining Buddha were basic and dark, which was a blessing for reasons I'll not elaborate on here, but they served their purpose.

Two hours later we were all huddled together in the truck en route back to Mawlamyine. I spent my time counting trucks overtaking us, with a driver casually texting while undertaking this perilous procedure. Pleased to report we made it back without incident. After a short break Chris led us up the hill in town to visit The Kyaikthanlan pagoda which was a wonderful viewpoint from which to enjoy the setting sun bouncing off the golden peaks of the pagoda. The pagoda itself was impressive, even for those travel-weary tourists who already have a few hundred pagodas under their belt. It was built in 875 AD during the reign of Mon King Mutpi Raja. Rudyard Kipling is believed to have written his famous *Lookin' lazy at the sea* line from The Road to Mandalay poem at this very pagoda. He must not have been looking at the sea only as he also wrote "I should better remember what the pagoda was like should I not have fallen deeply and irrevocably in love with a Burmese girl at the foot of the first flight of steps..."

Walking back down the hill to the hotel, negotiations commenced as to preferred venues for dinner that evening. When I'm just travelling with Les, I know how fraught these discussions could be. We knew that there was a night market somewhere in Mawlamyine. Even with the benefit of GPS, we were unsuccessful in finding it so settled upon a Chinese restaurant a short distance from the hotel.

I remember how dark it was in the middle of town, with limited street lighting which increased the likelihood of being hit by a car or tripping over a sleeping dog.

Les – 3 February 2020

I was familiar with Chris's concept of a rest day. Not for him the dull prospect of lazing by the pool, having a leisurely lunch, a quiet snooze and perhaps a stroll to the market before dinner.

I could imagine him smilingly explaining the options, 'We can ride to the museum and then visit a cave. Oh and for those who are interested, there's a temple about 20 kms, (this usually means nearer 30), away. It's not a very steep hill'.

Sometimes though, places of local interest were too far or perhaps too isolated even for Chris to consider cycling so in these cases, to avoid boredom (heaven forbid) setting in, he would organise transport of some kind. Myanmar is not the sort of place where you're going to find a limo service so this invariably means up to ten people piling into a van of some kind with seating for four at best. And that doesn't include the driver and his assistant.

MAWLAMYINE TO THANBYUZAYAT
4 FEBRUARY 2020

An early departure, Tuesday morning, was required if we were to secure boat transportation while the tide was high. A tickly throat the previous evening had now morphed into a runny nose and I was nervous. Had I just picked up a cold or something more sinister? I knew that if I had coronavirus, I might infect my bike buddies. As an Australian, there was also the prospect of spending two weeks on Christmas Island in quarantine on the way back to Brisbane. Despite the lovely name of the island, it houses a notorious detention centre where I would be a *guest*. Both of these outcomes were cause for nightmares.

We left shortly after six so it was still relatively cool. I always enjoy the first two hours in the saddle, and it was an enjoyable 37 kilometre ride along Mawlamyine's coast, despite my increasing sneezing and sniffling. We passed monks patiently collecting their morning's alms and villagers buying supplies at markets beside the pagodas. It was wonderful to see the many innovative ways that bikes had been converted into cargo carrying vehicles.

There were also children on bikes decked out in immaculately pressed, long sarongs with crisp white shirts. Our arrival in the fishing village attracted attention with locals emerging from their huts on stilts to check out the curious collective of cyclists. There appeared to be confusion over the number of boats that had been requested for the journey to Kyaikkhami, so while Chris commenced negotiations, the rest of us perused snacks hanging in plastic bags and purchased beverages. After a while we were led down to the river's edge where two old, timber fishing boats sat rocking quietly. I could not see how ten cyclists with their bikes and chattels could comfortably fit on board, and indeed while we did all obtain a space, no one was comfortable.

I secured a spot next to the driver controlling the outboard motor attached to a long metal rod, while my compatriots lay *spoon like* across the bow, under the shade of a timber slab. For a while the two boats were tied together, but this became perilous when one of my compatriots rolled around trying to get more comfortable, causing the boats to dangerously rock. With communication a problem and no one having a life vest, there was a quick scramble to untie the ropes connecting the vessels. The potential problem was blissfully oblivious to most of my compatriots who were soundly asleep.

With the danger of subsiding averted, we continued to chug up the river. I had visions of Katherine Hepburn and Humphrey Bogart on the African Queen imagining myself as a great explorer in an unknown land. However, there was limited wild life apart from a few birds and hardly any people on land that regularly floods.

Two hours later, we pulled into a long rocky pier where the process of disembarking began. Our bikes and goods were wheeled and carried up to a large lean-to café. I was sunburnt but pleased to be back on solid ground. Chris went off with the fisherman and beverages, to sit at an outside table where price negotiations continued. They were still wanting to charge us the same price for three boats as for two and Chris was having none of it. While the negotiations were underway outside, inside we watched a dubbed version of a Mr Bean cartoon on a projector with one highly amused child. It seems that British humour does travel! Twenty minutes later everyone emerged smiling when a price had been agreed and our transportation bill paid.

Kyaikkhami was for a short period the capital of British Lower Burma, before that responsibility was taken over by Mawlamyine. It is situated on a peninsula, 48 kilometres south of Mawlamyine. The town was largely deserted when we arrived. We needed to eat and there were ten restaurants sitting empty, side by side. Choosing the best one for lunch, was like playing the lottery. We chose the venue where we were warmly greeted. Unfortunately, the food was fatty, gristly and expensive by local standards. This was fortunately a rare occurrence on the trip. Most of the food is styled similarly to Thai food, although less spicy.

We were lucky that the town had a famous pagoda that Chris wanted us to visit. According to legend, the pagoda was located where a Buddha image washed ashore after floating on a raft from Sri Lanka. Yele pagoda dates from the 19th century and contains some of Buddha's hairs, but only men are allowed to visit the main altar where the hairs are located. This was the pagoda where all men needed to wear longyis, while the women wore sarongs. This was again appreciated by other visitors who encouraged us to sit with them for photos. The pagoda certainly had a lovely outlook and I enjoyed the different viewpoints looking out across the water.

We had a final 26 kilometre ride to Thanbyuzayat during the hottest part of the afternoon. I don't remember the ride so must have expunged it from my memory. I do however remember arriving at a designated rendezvous point at the Thanbyuzayat prisoner of war cemetery feeling knackered. Thanbyuzayat was where the infamous Burma - Siam railroad began. It was a massive project led by the Japanese and resulted in the deaths of 13,000 prisoners of war and also an estimated 80,000-100,000 civilians who were mainly forced labour brought from Malaya, the Dutch East Indies, or were conscripted in Siam (Thailand) and Burma (Myanmar). There are over 3,000 prisoners of war buried here including 1,651 British, 1,335 Australians, 621 Dutch, 15 Indian Army; 3 New Zealanders and one Canadian (Dermott-Powell, 1996).

It was now 3:00pm and the sun was at its most vicious. My cold was progressing and I was feeling miserable and ready for a shower. At this point Chris reported that the accommodation for the night was a little basic. Warning signs went off in my head and I inwardly groaned. On arrival, the Family World Hotel didn't look so bad. We were a bit out of town so it was quiet. There was a swimming pool and a ping pong table. Certainly, the bathroom wasn't very clean and the tiny synthetic towel provided didn't so much absorb water, as spread it more evenly over your body. The air-conditioning unit sounded like the engine of a 747 prior to take off – but it worked, and there was a charming sign inside saying 'Please switch off the fun when the electricity come low.' Yep. Not too bad, but Areeya and I were lucky. Six men were accommodated in a bunk house arrangement sharing one bathroom. My heart went out to them, particularly as there were reported to be several sonic snorers.

I washed my clothes and collapsed on to the bed for a much-needed nap. I was woken by Chris at dusk letting me know we were heading off to the war museum. I really wanted to pike out as I was tired, but I rolled off the bed, and reshoed my feet.

The Death War Museum was closed by the time we arrived, but this was a minor distraction for Chris. He'd discovered that the owner of the hotel next door is also the museum manager so was cajoled into opening it up for us. It's a modest museum, which ran old VCR videos from the war period on a flickering TV screen and had drawings and paintings created by artists-in- training which made the images they portrayed less violent. I'd already visited two war museums in Kanchanabri in Thailand so was familiar with the atrocities of the period.

It was now dark and we saddled up for another ride to the centre of town. Not all our bikes had lights. That was probably OK because neither did many of the cars on the road. They did however have horns which they used generously. This was probably the most dangerous part of the trip as the traffic had not abated. We crossed the road as a pack, for safety.

Thanbyuzayat did not have much to commend itself. It struck me as a town built for vehicles with people as a minor consideration. I guess this is not surprising as it was built as a tin mining centre. We found somewhere to eat beside a busy roundabout with trucks rolling past, with music screeching out from monstrous speakers and with signs we couldn't read. It appeared to be a protest. We found a place making hamburgers served curiously with three chips only. They were delicious, possibly because lunch had been so disappointing. We made it back to the Family World Hotel without incident and I collapsed into bed, barely noticing the outside street light blaring in. I slept soundly and woke to the gentle humming of monks and the sound of Areeya sniffling. I'd spread the lurgy.

Les – 4 February 2020

My back is mending nicely and I'm tempted into the gym for some light aerobic exercise followed by even lighter weights work. Checking the bike trip itinerary, I pretend I've joined them on the 26 kilometre ride to Thanbyuzayat as I pedal along on the gym's stationary bike. I've got my headphones on and the aircon is working well, an ample supply of chilled water is available. Just like being there really.

After my gym session I relax with a cold beer and enjoy my dinner watching another rerun of Star Trek before retiring to my comfortable queen-size bed. Yep, it's just like being there.

THANBYUZAYAT TO YE
5 FEBRUARY 2020

It's Wednesday morning, fifth of February as I dictate this while standing on Thanbyuzayat station waiting with the others to catch a train part way to Ye. We've been told the train is at least an hour late and Jeanine has led a troupe off to find food for the journey. Areeya is taking photos of me while Chris and Manu are chatting to a local who has welcomed the opportunity to practice his English. This curious chap shows us the tracks where the Burma rail started and the crumbling, colonial-style house fifty metres away where the Japanese commander overseeing the construction of the railway, lived.

Some of my bored chums are being silly on the railway lines, taking photos in dangerous positions. We're lucky that we have good visibility in both directions and that the infrequently arriving trains, do so slowly.

Several monks squat in the sunshine and a dozen ladies with their faces brightly painted with thanakha, arrive with large tin plates on their heads, piled with food and drinks. I can see roasted corn husks, bags of noodles and mini towers of polystyrene carrying something warm. An old train, painted in blue and maroon, slowly approaches and the ladies go to work before the train stops selling their produce through open carriage windows to customers inside. There's a frenetic hive of activity for a minute until a whistle blows and all trading stops, and the ladies step back from the railway tracks. It's wonderful theatre.

We know that we will have our own dramatic production when our train finally arrives as there will be one minute only to load all bikes, panniers and cyclists. Jeannine, Areeya and I are allocated to the transport of the panniers while the men stand at the end of the platform with the bikes. It's a challenging job as the bikes are heavy and there is some distance to lift them up into the cargo carriage. With the help of a railway employee we're successful and are soon bouncing and swaying along, en route to Lamaing in the direction of Ye. Indeed, the train is a wonderful, old rattler and we have to hang on as we slide around on the timber seats. Everyone is laughing. Care needs to be taken not to put one's head outside as we swish past trees. This train is not of the bullet variety. It's the slowest train in Myanmar and possibly the world, traversing the 60 kilometres between Thanbyuzayat and Lamaing, in three hours. It's a wonderful way to see the countryside and locals going about their daily life, using the train to carry their wares and livestock.

Due to the lack of facilities at Thanbyuzayat station, I'm in need of a bathroom visit. It's a long time until we reach Lamaing, so I bravely visit the tiny room at the end of the carriage. Conveniently, there's a metal bar provided for customers to grasp, as they squat and swing. The constant movement makes it difficult to focus on the task at hand, but I'm ultimately successful with only slightly damp shoes.

Disembarking at Lamaing also requires careful coordination due to the limited stopping time. We drop the panniers out through the windows, testing everyone's catching skills while the bikes are hurriedly downloaded onto the platform.

We ride out from the station taking narrow roads and dirt tracks covered in the familiar red dust. It's only a few hundred meters until we come to a temple (of course). In addition to an impressive collection of golden pagodas, this temple featured a fifty-foot-tall monk onto which wasps had built an impressive nest, on the chin, which looks incongruously like a beard. Buddhist monks never have beards, because of the monastic disciplinary rules laid down by the Buddha. I quietly wondered if someone somewhere is having a private joke.

We are soon back on our bikes, on narrow dirt paths framed by tall palm trees. Piles of small blue rocks began to appear on the path and we are soon passing road construction gangs who eye us cautiously. The narrow path turns into a long sea of crumbly blue gravel, bogging our tyres. There's no verge on which to ride and avoid the quagmire. One of the workers catches Areeya's attention and calls her over for a chat. We are fortunate that Thai is so widely spoken.

After consultation, Areeya tells us that it would be more polite for us to push, rather than ride our bikes through the blue gravel. We all comply and it is only another one hundred metres until the road again becomes a bumpy dirt track. The group begins to disperse at this stage, with some more confidently navigating the rough road than others. I have to keep stopping as my water bottle keeps bouncing off. Manu has his brakes fail on the rugged terrain and comes off in a sea of dust. He is soon joined by other cyclists and a policeman, who emerges seemingly, out of thin air. The discussion which follows makes some of the cyclists uneasy.

I have this part of the story recounted to me later, as I'm waiting with Chris and a few others in a shady spot further along. We all stop at the next village, to attend to repairs and to have a drink. We're a major curiosity and many villagers gather round to watch us. Foreigners are rare in this part of Myanmar and I realise that I haven't seen another since Mawlamyine.

The police suddenly arrive, and with the assistance of a young boy no older than eight, acting as interpreter, enquires about our travel plans in a melange of English and Thai.

'Where you go?'

We confirm we aren't staying in the village, we're only stopping for refreshments and repairs and that we are booked into an *official hotel* in Ye for the night. The fear of deportation soon dissipates.

Manu is still suffering, not only from the fall but because of the dust which he could not get out of his eyes. One of the villagers secures a bottle of saline, which does the trick.

They are generous folk and refuse payment. As we ride out of town some villagers run along beside us handing out bottles of water and a short distance along we are waved down by a woman at a small stall inviting us to enjoy her deep fried, coconut pancakes. I'm not sure if the villagers feel upset by our encounter with the immigration police or were simply generous people.

At the next refreshment stop, we were told that the rest of journey to Ye would be on the main road which was hilly and busy. Areeya invites those interested in skipping this part of the journey to take a tuk tuk. We will of course miss visiting another very big Buddha. For me, this seals the deal. I join Jeannine, Manu and Teerayud in squeezing into the alternate transport to Ye. There are young lads practicing Thai boxing in the front courtyard of the Mya Myint Mo Hotel when we arrive. The hotel is well located, with warm water and cold air-conditioning so all my basic needs are met. I wash my clothes, grateful for the two-night stop which makes it easier to get everything dry.

We eat dinner at the *Dream Restaurant* conveniently located a block away from the hotel. There is a huge screen showing an attractive girl with hair blowing in the wind, singing a song like thousands of other aspiring pop stars around the world. I don't understand the words but it doesn't matter. Some things are universal. Over a delicious bowl of noodles served with Tiger beers, we learn that the big Buddha at Banana Mountain (Ko Yin Lay) had indeed been impressive. Chris kindly makes plans for the four *pikers* to visit the Buddhist complex first thing tomorrow morning.

Les – 5 February 2020

I love trains. I dream of a future where hyper fast trains travel, probably via vacuum underground tunnels, around the globe, reaching speeds of 4000kms and taking me from London to Sydney in a few hours without the need to squeeze into a cramped aeroplane seat.

I imagined the train my cycling pals were taking would be a far cry from my futuristic dream and it was bound to be late. But even so, I envied them their 3 hour, 20km an hour (about my favourite cycling speed), journey.

Not to feel too left out I took a ferry ride on the Brisbane river and gazed at the local inhabitants on the nearby path, dressed in their tight-fitting athletic clothes, fascinated and frequently aghast at their gaudy full limb tattoos and prominent body piercings.

YE TO BIN LE WA
6 FEBRUARY 2020

It was indeed impressive. Banana Mountain was a huge Buddhist complex and even the mini-van driver wasn't sure where to drop us. We selected a high view point and disembarked arranging to meet again at the bottom in an hour. A woman sweeping leaves pointed to our shoes - which we removed. Jeannine immediately stepped in rooster droppings. I could hear the blighter crowing and saw him watching us from a nearby wall. He was mocking us.

The complex comprised not one, but four massive Buddhas sitting back to back. For scale, they were as high as a nine-story building. Additionally, there was a giant reclining Buddha. The views from the site were impressive with green vegetation and gentle rolling hills as far as the eye could see. The inside of the Buddhas had also been designed to inspire feelings of awe. I was pleased that Chris provided time for us to visit and I'd encourage others to do the same.

While we'd been up the mountain the others had been watching a parade of children immaculately decked out in red uniforms. The occasion for the parade was the Mon National Day. The Mon flags were everywhere while Myanmar flags could not be seen.

There was a moment of panic prior to departure for Bin Le Wa when Jeannine realised she'd left her money sack in the minivan which had taken us up to Banana Mountain. The hotel owner immediately hopped in his truck and returned twenty minutes later with the lost item. Emergency averted. He refused to accept a tip for his kindness in retrieving the sack. Indeed, I was taken by the helpfulness and generosity of locals everywhere we visited.

Originally there were two options for the day. Option One was visiting the Juan Yua village which had a mix of Mon and Karen inhabitants. From here, we'd take a boat up the Ye river where Chris has promised crystal waters, ideal for swimming. Sounded lovely. Unfortunately, there was ongoing fighting between the Myanmar and the Mon National Liberation armies so we went with plan B which was a ride to Bin Le Wa beach.

Our exit from town via the main road was busy but unremarkable. Suddenly our indomitable leader turned left off the main road onto a narrow concrete path. It was great to be away from the pre second world war vehicles rattling past us at lightning speed.

My pleasure at our taking a quieter path, quickly dissipated as we started passing burning piles of rubbish and the concrete path changed to a sandy quagmire. The smoke and piles of rubbish grew higher. I dismounted again, squinting furiously, before pushing my bike forward through the ever-thickening greyish haze. I suddenly saw the benefits of having a cold as I couldn't identify all the fruity scents, and pulled out another tissue from my rapidly diminishing supply. I blew my nose, remounted the bike and soldiered on.

Our diversion was blissfully short and we were all soon bouncing along dirt roads through fishing villages, returning the smiles and waves of curious onlookers. We arrived at the Bin Le Wa beach and all forgot our irritation at Chris' short cut through the rubbish tip. A gentle breeze restored our spirits and we enjoyed a seafood feast of fried fish, tempura prawns and tea-leaf salad, followed by a long leisurely slumber on timber slats in the shade.

Our avocado shakes were served by a beautiful girl with a giggly baby dangling from her hip. When she smiled, her beauty was somewhat diminished by a set of teeth which looked like sunset at Stonehenge. Like many locals, she was a fan of betel nut and clearly had been for some time. Her lips were stained crimson and her teeth had broken and crumbled. Like all the women we met, she was a model of elegance in her beautiful sarong. We met her partner who was missing the bottom half of his right leg. Motorcycle accident we were told. This news surprised no one as we frequently saw entire families on motorbikes, without helmets.

I'd played with the idea of dipping into the Andaman sea. From a distance it looked so inviting. Closer up examination revealed multiple plastic bags, broken glass and poly styrofoam casing. On the sand itself there were cow and dog droppings and I wasn't clear on where the effluent from the local village might be ending up. I decided that caution was the best choice and hoped that the beach waters will be attended to at some stage as it is otherwise a picture-perfect location. I sat and read while Jean, Jeannine and Chris visited a nearby village where fish were drying on long racks on the beach. My phone pinged showing a photo of a nearby pagoda that Chow was visiting. His enthusiasm for every temple was commendable

As the sun and temperature began to drop it was time to ride back to the town of Ye where we were staying for the night. Chris avoided our wrath by choosing the main road into town. As we joined everyone else speeding along, I witnessed a huge sack of something very heavy, fall off a small truck in front of us and wondered if, on the route through the rubbish tip we had increased by tenfold, the likelihood of arriving at our destination unscathed.

We arrived back in Ye late afternoon. While the others went off in search of avocado milkshakes and ice-cream, I was in urgent need of replenishing my dwindling supply of tissues. After the fourth store had smiled and said no, I resigned myself to having to buy toilet paper which was not a great option being bulky to carry and scratchy on my tender nose. Luckily the fifth store we visited had supplies and I was delighted to secure 12 small packs. Areeya had caught a bus to Dawei that morning as she needed to get back to Thailand to receive guests at Hidden Holiday House. She texted me that there was a wonderful spa in Dawei. The thought of a long soak and massage at the end of the journey, and the opportunity to wash away all the red dust, filled me with joy. My thoughts were interrupted by the pinging of the phone with my colleagues sharing photos of a nearby carnival come night market.

The carnival reminded me of the Newcastle show I visited as a teenager. Pink fairy floss stalls everywhere, children screaming as they slipped down giant slides, gaudy disco music bursting out through tinny speakers. I could hear my husband complaining loudly in my ear, even though he wasn't with us. There were stores selling tit-tat, like glow in the dark sticks and novelty hats. Deep fryers were working overtime and kebabs were sizzling on BBQs. I enjoyed roti with chickpeas cooked by a lady in a ditch on the side of the road. I like chickpeas and felt sorry for her poor market position. I followed this later by noodles with vegetables from a stall in the main market area, that had tables chairs. I only chose this dish because there was somewhere to sit. I'm not a fan of eating while walking. There were a few other foreigners at the fair. I was amused to see a young European guy, being trailed by six local girls. He was clearly the key attraction for them.

The clamour began to grate on me so I returned to the hotel. The sounds from the carnival could still be heard from my room. However, they were preferable to the person in the room beside me who was expectorating flamboyantly. There were also many people in the hotel smoking, which for me as an Australian, is a habit that's practically outlawed. Indeed, I was surprised to see how common smoking was with little kiosks conveniently located on main roads, selling either cigarettes or betel nut. I really wanted to get a good night's sleep as we had an early start the following morning. I could feel the likelihood of this, slipping away.

Les – 6 February 2020

Just another day for me. Morning walk in the park followed by a stretch. Another physio visit today after which, to vary things a bit and because I have nothing but time, I decide to walk the few kilometres home via 'The Valley'.

Fortitude Valley is about as close as the rather staid city of Brisbane gets to having a bohemian or art district. There are a number of clubs catering for dancers, drinkers and other delights, all closed in the late morning as I strolled passed. Chinese, Thai and Vietnamese restaurants abound and there are quite a few simple old fashioned pubs, all reasonably busy with sad looking lonely drinkers at this early hour. The Valley is also home to a number of shops selling adventure wear which I like to frequent from time to time, to stock up on my favourite brands. Not that I plan any adventure travel in the near future but I like to dress for it, just in case. I wander in to one or two and check out the sale items before returning home.

YE TO SAN HLAN
7 FEBRUARY 2020

I'm recording this in bed. The dreadful music from the market backslash carnival-from-hell, continued until midnight. I dozed fitfully being woken by people in the next room speaking loudly with occasional hacking. I was tempted to shush them but appreciated they may be experiencing the effects of too much betel nut. When the music started again at five this morning, it was accompanied by the howls of the hound next door to the hotel. My cold seemed worse but probably just because of my sleep deprived state.

The bikes and panniers were again precariously loaded on the top of two minivans for the 185 kilometre journey to a point not far from the village of San Hlan. The driver was indifferent about securing the load, so I insisted that all panniers were secured with ropes and bicycle straps. I'd frequently seen goods flyoff the back of trucks and didn't fancy arriving at our destination *sans luggage*.

It was a busy and dangerous road with no verge and I pitied the three guys who rode all the way on the previous trip. We came to a checkpoint on the border between the Mon state and the Tanintharyi Region where passports were handed over and checked. The guards warmly remembered Chris and Chow from when they had ridden through on the Tough Nut Bike Tour. There were smiles and shaking hands and a contribution made to 'coffee money' for the border guards to ensure a smooth passage through on the next tour's passage. There were two other security check points before we entered the town of Dawei.

It was a long and boring journey and Chris attempted a stop for lunch. The driver said fine and started unloading the bags indicating he was leaving. He was not going to stay and wait for us as he had another long drive ahead of him. Negotiations were undertaken and the bags were again thrown on top of the minivan – without being secured. I again climbed up the ladder pointing at the ropes and bicycle straps that needed to be used. We all piled back into the minivans, grateful for the break, albeit a short one.

The road became narrower and after a slow climb up a long hill, the vans stopped and all bikes and chattels were dismounted. We were all keen to ride having been cooped up like sardines. It was a wonderful five kilometre downward descent into the San Hlan village. As I gripped my brakes for dear life I wondered if this was the only road into town, as I did not fancy riding up this hill the following day.

San Hlan is a fishing community on a small bay. We rode through the centre of the village to reach a beautiful timber guest house, built on rocks at the water's edge. It'd been built as a community project to generate revenue and it was charming. I can hear monks chanting and the water lapping against the rocks as I record these impressions. In front of me are young Burmese tourists, crawling over the rocks taking selfies. All rooms have a mattress on the floor covered by a mosquito net and there's a large, open bathroom connected to each room. There's a wonderful view out to the fishing boats bobbing in the bay.

Lunch was delicious and included one of my favourite Thai dishes, gai phat kaphrao consisting of fried chicken, chilly, garlic and basil rice with a fried egg on top. There were puppies nipping at our feet as we ate and those who didn't close their bedroom door that night, were woken with wet feet from the same scoundrels. After lunch we walked up the beach, watching young girls carrying huge sacks of produce from the boats to a storage shed. It reminded me of a previous trip I'd taken to Nepal where girls often carried two to three travellers' luggage, secured only by bands around their forehead. The girls giggled effusively as we took photos. Further along, young boys were playing soccer (football) on the sand. At the end of the beach under the shade of palm trees, sat a woman and her daughter repairing a fishing net. She spoke Thai so Chris was able to discover that she had previously been working in Mae Sot, but needed to return to San Hlan when her husband, a fisherman, had drowned. None of the boats we had travelled on in Myanmar had life vests and indeed there is a casual concern for safety both on the water, and on the road. I know my perspective is influenced by my upbringing in Australia where there is strict, and at times zealous, attention to safety rules.

As we walked back through the village, we could hear a hear a gentle thud as a couple made fish paste using a timber paddle rammed into a pot. It had a distinctive smell. There was also the screechy sound of birds which we soon realised was mainly a recording, as a 'swiftlet house' had been constructed where birds were encouraged to nest. The birds' nest would ultimately become the principal ingredient in a soup of the same name.

Over Tiger beers that night, I asked Chris about the route to be taken out of the village the following morning.

'There's only one road.'

'Transportation requested please.' Three of my compatriots were also not interested in making the ascent out of town by bike so we were to be loaded into a tiny truck and transported to the top of the hill to wait for the others.

∼

Les – 7 February 2020

Noise pollution is a common problem everywhere these days. Living in a city centre apartment has its advantages for sure but one of the main downsides is noisy inconsiderate neighbours. I lay in bed while boisterous drunken guests in the apartment next door shouted at each other on the nearby balcony. Finally, I decided to take action and filled out an online form our building has created to alert the security guard. The affable Ezekiel soon sorted out the issue and I drifted off planning to play my Led Zeppelin collection as loud as possible, early the following morning. I didn't. I'm not that petty.

SAN HLAN TO DAWEI
8 FEBRUARY 2020

Ensconced within the safety of the mosquito netting, I slept reasonably well last night. I say *reasonably well* because it soon became obvious that like the screech of the swiftlets, the monks chanting was also playing on a continuous loop. The monastery was on the other side of the bay, but sound travelled. There was also the pitter patter of the puppies running up and down the timber decking. My cold had now moved from my nose to my chest. I crossed my fingers that it would be gone before I boarded a flight home, now only three days away.

Four of us loaded into a tiny truck laden with our bikes and panniers, and the panniers of a few of our colleagues who weren't interested in riding all the way to the top carrying their stuff. Apart from the initial climb, today was a gentle 31 kilometre ride into Dawei.

We stopped at the first village we came to for breakfast. It was run by a family who unfortunately didn't speak Thai, Chinese or English. Chris never lets a little thing like a lack of a common language get in the way. We enjoyed a delicious dish of noodle soup with pork (I think). Riding along we stopped to take photos of a gorgeous black and white mural of Aung San Suu Kyi on a bus stop. Ten kilometres along we stopped for freshly made sugar cane juice and iced coffee. Nestle seems to have a monopoly on these beverages wherever we stopped.

Getting closer to town, we again dismounted, this time to visit the Tanintharyi Cultural Museum. There were a number of spectacular paintings and information about local industries. I was particularly interested in the textiles/fabric industry displays. I'd planned on going sarong shopping as soon as we had checked into the hotel in Dawei. There was also information about local festivals including,

- Pouring water to Nga-Khone-Ma (a kind of fish)
- Inviting rain by male and female frogs dancing
- Buffalo fighting festival
- Alms-food bowl floating festival
- Twenty-eight Buddha images wandering and worshipping festival

I was particularly sorry we wouldn't be in town to see the *male and female frog dancing festival.* However, there was the Hindu Thaipusam festival in full swing when we finally made it into town.

As we were departing the museum, a guy on a passing motorcycle stopped for a chat with Chris resulting in a curious invitation for a ride with the Dawei cycling group at 5:00am the following morning. We could hear the beating of drums and shrill of whistles as we entered the outskirts of the city. Getting closer we could watch the full singing and dancing spectacle. Many colourfully decorated carts greeted us, transporting effigies of Ganesh, the elephant-headed Hindu god of beginnings. They were accompanied by men wearing magnificent white and gold sarongs and elaborately decorated elephants. It took a moment to recognise that these elephants were actors performing a wonderful pantomime, delighting children and adults alike.

Dawei is a large town with multiple markets displaying kaleidoscopic coloured clothes and fabrics making it hard to concentrate on safely weaving our bikes around tuk-tuks and minivans as we rode to the charmingly named, Best House Hotel. After a quick shower we all piled into two tuk-tuks for the short journey to the Tavoy Kitchen. We could have walked but it was really hot and the pavements were very narrow. I remember that the service at the cafe was very slow but we were in no hurry and my tea leaf salad was delicious and worth waiting for. The dry ingredients for my now most favourite dish in Myanmar were for sale in packets at the hotel's reception. However I knew that there was a 50/50 chance that it would be confiscated when I passed through immigration. Australian border control is very strict about food coming into the country with multiple signs warning of a $50,000 fine for those attempting to do so.

We returned to the hotel early afternoon. I'd abandoned the idea of visiting the spa that Areeya had recommended as my cold was still hanging on. Instead I went fabric shopping. It was so difficult to limit myself to only two pieces of the magic cloth. They had the most beautiful collection of colours and designs I'd ever seen. If we'd been staying longer than one night, I could have had skirts and tops made. Next time! On my way back to the Best House, I passed a wedding party having their photos taken. Everyone was wearing outfits of apricot satin, even the male attendants resplendent in their apricot sarongs and matched with apricot thongs on their feet. They signalled for me to come over and chat, welcoming the opportunity to practice their English.

This was our last night in Myanmar so a special restaurant had been selected for the occasion. It was the Pale Eikari restaurant which Chris had found though a recommendation on the website Travel Fish. This was our goto place for local information throughout the trip. I was amused by the duck feet options, much to the curiosity of my cycling buddy Tseng who considered it a perfectly normal menu:

- Boneless duck feet (deep fried)
- Boneless duck feet with oyster sauce
- Boneless duck feet with kalian
- Boneless duck feet with chop meal
- Salad duck feet

Thinking about it, it was no different to getting potato on the side with everything in Ireland.

After a couple of beers, Manu announced that this would be the last cycling trip he would be joining us for. He'd decided that cycling 20 kilometres a day in the heat, was his limit, so unless there was a soft, soft nut tour scheduled in the future, he would be bowing out. Manu is the oldest of our party at 71 and had been a regular on Chris's tours for the last twelve years. I have a feeling that Chris will be able to accommodate this requirement for future rides. We toasted Manu and Chris then asked who would be up for a 5:00am ride with the Dawei Cycling club. Knowing there was a long day ahead, squeezed into the back of a truck utility, I cautiously lifted my hand.

Les – 8 February 2020

Walk. Physio. Bike ride. Netflix. Read. Music. Bed.

DAWEI TO HUAY PLU
9 FEBRUARY 2020

It was pitch black at 5:00am the following morning when Chow and myself joined Chris in the hotel car park. The designated meeting spot for the cycle was conveniently located around the corner. It was easy to spot the other cyclists uniformly wearing their local club's jersey, with matching socks, gloves and helmets. They viewed us curiously, and there was an initial language problem because the person who had invited us had not yet arrived and none of the other riders spoke English, Thai or Chinese. I'm sure they were thinking,

'Who the heck are these strange foreigners and why on earth are they cycling in such casual clothes?'

Chris and Chow were wearing shorts and t-shirts with plastic slippers and Crocs respectively on their feet. It was strangely awkward. Luckily a cyclist arrived a few minutes later who spoke Malay and was able to chat with Chow and get the background on who we were and why we were there.

There were nervous smiles and nods and at 5:10am, fifteen of us mounted our steeds and rode out of town. It was wonderfully cool and I was thrilled to be off on a new adventure.

However, as we left town we rode into darkness save for the small beam from the bike lights. It made me appreciate how much I valued seeing the surface of the road. I had my fingers crossed I didn't hit a pot hole or sleeping dog. From time to time a car passed illuminating the road for the next twenty metres, but we were soon again in darkness. The car lights also revealed that we were riding through a fog of dust. I needed to push those pedals more than I was used to, in order to keep up with the peloton. No plans had been finalised between the three of us as to how long we would cycle with the club, who were headed south for the town of Thayetchaung, 30 kilometre away. Luckily, after 9kms, we arrived at the Shin Mothtee pagoda where we waved goodbye to our new biking buddies.

Chris and Chow went inside while I watched a woman gently sweeping leaves, and regarded the curious and at times brutal paintings on the passageway to the temple. It seemed incongruous to have such violent images at a place of worship. As we rode back into Dawei I could see Chris pointing at a building and we pulled into a busy tea house. Myanmar is famous for their tea houses as a place for family, business, politics, and of course, tea. They're more popular with older folk as the younger generation prefers modern style cafes. This tea house was family oriented with groups of 6 – 8 squatting on plastic chairs around tiny tables on the terrace with workers chatting convivially on long tables inside. We took a place at the far end of one table. I could hear people coughing and the woman behind the cash register had bits of fabric stuck up her nose, which didn't fill me with confidence.

There were half a dozen small pastries on a plate. They looked cold and unappetising and I'm not sure how long they'd been there. I took a bite out of a curry paste samosa which was very nice. I also tried a round fried pastry something which had sweet bean paste inside. It was less to my liking. There was a man walking round pouring tea into the cup, splashing into the saucer. I'd seen this before on my last visit to Myanmar and knew it was intentional. My morning tea custom is more sedate so I poured myself a cup of Chinese tea from the pot on the table. I'm aware that eating pastries for breakfast is not consistent with my plan for losing weight. However, I'm keeping well within budget with breakfast costing us 1,000 kyat or $1 Aussie dollar.

Back to the hotel for a shower and pack. I inwardly groan as I look in the mirror at my increasingly grey and tatty hair. Oh well. What does it matter? I'm looking forward to being back at Hidden Holiday House tonight. I focus on this rather than the next four hours, steeling myself for the trip ahead. Chris has indicated that the return journey would make the original entry into Myanmar, seem like a pleasant stroll by the pond. Significant attention was paid to ensuring that anything that could possibly come off the bikes was removed and the panniers were roped together securely in the back. I put on my mask as I squeezed into the back seat. My cold was on the way out, but I wanted to be careful.

The first 50 of the 135 kilometre journey were on a wonderful sealed road and were scenic. Surely Chris had been exaggerating? Suddenly the bitumen ended and we were on pot-holed and dusty roller coaster ride. After two minutes on this new section of road, I wished I'd kept my bike helmet on, as with every bump, my head bashed against the roof. Music blasting from the car CD player completed the surreal experience. Still. Everyone smiled. Well, initially at least. We were on our way.

A first break from the uncomfortable ride came at a Karen check point. I took a photo of the Great Tenasserim River that we were skirting along, and was told to put the camera away as photos were not allowed.

There were few occasions when the scenery was interesting and it was hard enough to see through the sea of dust. After two hours of dipping, swinging and narrowly missing slipping into the gorge at one particularly precarious bridge crossing, we made it to the half way point and the only restaurant/stopping place en route. I uncoiled myself from the utility, feeling like I'd been in a tumble dryer. It was good to stretch my legs before the final assault. I was intrigued to learn that Jean in the second utility, had managed to sleep all the way. I was envious and confounded. How was this possible?

We climbed back into the utilities for on the final stretch and two hours later we arrived at a shanty town called Htee Kee on the Myanmar border. It reminded me of the towns that cowboys would ride into town in western movies, sandy and deserted. The accommodation was however of a lower standard, with most houses constructed of corrugated iron.

The Myanmar immigration processing centre however, was built of timber and gyprock and reminded me of the old weather shed at school. We weren't allowed to take photos inside, which was a pity as the process had a comical sense to it – as we shuffled forward, playing musical chairs along a row of tiny plastic stools. Our passports were duly stamped by a bored agent. I came outside into the scorching heat to secure my panniers and inspect my bike. I'd lost my bell with an Australian flag and there were a few scrapes to the paintwork. Otherwise, my bike was OK. I perused my surroundings while waiting for the rest of the troupe to get processed. There was an ugly concrete construction underway on a distance hill. Another casino I was told. There were already four casinos in town serving the needs of Thai gamblers.

Sweating profusely, we mounted our bikes and headed down the hill to the next checkpoint 100 metres away. This was then followed by another checkpoint 20 metres later. I could see a concrete road in front of us dipping down. Yes. We'd be leaving the dust behind. I was also looking forward to entering this *terra nullius* or no man's land, which was a 4 kilometre stretch between Myanmar and Thailand. No sooner had I started my enthusiastic descent, taking care to swap from the right to left hand side of the road, when the first of three dogs emerged from nowhere objecting violently to me being on *their road*. I hate barking dogs. As I pushed down hard on the pedals seeking to outride these troublesome mutts, I could hear furious whistling from the top of the hill with my friends calling out for me to stop. Reluctantly I squeezed the brakes and turned by bike around. The hill was too steep for me to ride up when I was carrying panniers and I was delighted when one of the immigration guards simultaneously shoed the dogs away and took over the task of pushing my bike back up the hill. Loved this chivalrous behaviour. There was a cursory glance at my passport, I was asked where I was from and then bestowed a big smile. I was again free to start the downhill descent. On reflection I think that our cycling group was the most interesting thing happening that day in Htee Kee so the guards were keen to chat.

Once through Thai immigration we congregated at a lunch spot waiting for everyone to come through. Two of our party were taking a long time and finally David arrived saying that Tseng was having trouble. Chris went back to sort it out. The problem was that Tseng was Taiwanese which is a country not enjoying convivial relations with China. China has very close relationships with both Myanmar and Thailand. Because of this, on entering Myanmar Tseng had had his visa stamped on a piece of paper rather than in the passport itself. The border guards were now insisting that he made his way back to the original entry point near Mae Sot – which would involve re-doing the highway from hell and an additional four days by train or truck to get back to the starting point. And Tseng was booked to fly out from Bangkok airport (Suvarnabhumi) that night to Taipei, starting work the following day.

It was a real mission impossible moment and Chris was the Tom Cruise character, metaphorically hanging from the ceiling to rescue Tseng. He charmed the guards, (of course), and confirmed that the troublesome Tseng would be out of the country that night. They reluctantly stamped the piece of paper and threw the evidence away, thereby avoiding a diplomatic incident. We could see that the colour had drained from Tseng's face by the time he joined us.

After a lunch of my favourite Holy basil rice with fried chicken we commenced the 70 kilometre drive from the border to Kanchanaburi where we dropped off Teerayud and then a further 80 kilometres to Huay Plu. We picked up whiskey and snacks at the local 7/11 before arriving at Hidden Holiday House for a welcome shower followed by a lovely meal together.

Les – 9 February 2020

Knowing that today is the day Tracy will cross the border back into Thailand from Myanmar, I think back to the first real land border I ever crossed. This was from France to Italy on my tandem trip from Enfield to Athens. I'd crossed the channel many times of course, from England to France, but that entails a more gradual change from one country to the next. Baguettes are sold alongside chips on the ferry and people are speaking in a mixture of English and French.

Riding our rusting Raleigh between Menton and Ventimiglia in 1976 was my first experience of a direct land border crossing. Naively I imagined there would be a gradual change from one country to the next. Geographically I suppose this is the case as the hills of southern France become the hills of southern Italy. But culturally the change is of course immediate. Say au revoir to France and buongiorno to Italy and that's it. Road signs are in Italian. There are pasta and gelato stores and kiosks everywhere.

The coffee is better. People seem more outgoing and flamboyant. In 1976 even the money was different and what had been a simple mental calculation of roughly 10 francs to the pound became an Einsteinian display of advanced mathematics to work out whether 5000 lira was a lot to pay for a loaf of bread.

PART III

AT THE END OF THE JOURNEY

REFLECTING ON THE JOURNEY

We'd made it. Hidden Holiday House was journey's end. We'd avoided major accidents and being arrested so there was much to celebrate. We reflected on the best and worst of the journey while we emptied the whiskey bottle. I posed three questions:

What were the best bits of the trip?

What were the biggest challenges?

What words would you use to describe our leader?

BEST BITS

The things that everyone liked included the camaraderie of group, history and culture of Myanmar, mountain views, opportunity to experience village life and to admire the women and their striking sarongs. Here's what they told me.

Friendship

Friendship amongst the cyclists and with the people we met as we rode through their villages were frequently mentioned.

Tseng. Friendship is the best thing. Everyone is like a family.

. . .

Chow. I like this group because every member come from different country. Different people. Different languages. Yeah, most particular thing in this second group.

Tracy. This is a friendly and helpful group. And I think because we have all been together on a trip before. This makes it easier.

The history and culture of Myanmar

Tseng. Different local cultures of Burma were also the best thing. Because I am a Buddhist, I find the difference between Buddha statues in Burma and Thailand interesting. It solves the one problem of my meditation.

Jean. The first thing was the discovery of Burma. I have the impression that it's changing.

Jeannine. Our ability to 'travel in the past'. It's like you are travelling in a previous era.

Areeya. It's good that I have been to Burma before and many similar countries, but it was much more in terms of what I expected. Because in the history of Thailand and Burmese, sometimes there have been problems and I don't know how they feel about Thai people. And I was thinking about my packing and if I should show that I am Thai in my clothing. I want to see how they react to Thai people, a friend or whatever, but everybody happy. They welcome us.

So I always keep telling my friend and family in the Facebook how much I appreciated the Burmese people, they are very friendly and beautiful people and they appreciate our country.

Natural scenery and pagodas and temples

Manu. I know I travel slowly. I like of course to feel history when I travel. And very interesting for me was the temple at Kyaikkhami and the Kyaikthanlan pagoda in Mawlamyine from the time when George Orwell was there. This is the most important thing. Temples were one of the most important points of difference between South-East Asia and the influence of India arriving exactly from this point.

David. The huge Buddha thing at Banana Mountain where you made me walk up the stairs and I banged my head.

Jean and Chris. Banana mountain was the second thing for me. It makes you go wow. Both the entrance into the complex and the view from the top.

Jeannine. Scenery on the second day when we were cycling out of Hpa An. I liked the Kyuak Kalat pagoda on the rock, on the limestone pinnacle and we had lovely scenery and mountain views around us.

Village life

Tracy. I loved the easy smiles when we rode through villages, saying *mingalaba*. They seemed very pleased and entertained that we were traveling to see them. I also liked the sense of community in every village. You could easily see inside every house and people were out on the streets, eating dinner together in the evening at the market. A very communal lifestyle. When I think about my own town, everyone lives in their apartments and the doors are shut, and we all live our own lives. We are not a part of such a connected community. Every village was a part of a community.

Jeannine. I liked the fishing village – the one on the beach that we walked to from Bin Le Wa where we saw the fish drying.

San Hlan village

David. I think number three on my list of best things has to be the fishing village of San Hlan.

. . .

Chow. Best things like Sal Hlan village very much The scenery is just remind me about during 70s time of the Singapore and Hong Kong.

Jeannine. There was something very slow about it that I liked. Something we've lost. That's why we're again travelling in the past. 'La temps retrouve'.

Cycling

Tracy. I liked the first hour of cycling every day, when there was no pain and the temperature was cool.

Jeannine. I also liked the biking because it was not painful - but it was painful when I was walking.

Chow. Maybe for this trip the biking section is a bit too short for me.
  [Side note: Chow was a member of the Tough Nut Tour]
Yeah, yeah there was a certain time on the Tough Nut where I needed to rest a few times. It was a challenge to make it on time ride, but Soft Nut was too short for me.

Travelling by boats and trains

. . .

Manu. I liked our trip by fishing boat to Kyaikkhami. This was not a tourist boat.

Areeya. I like the mix of activities on the tour. Trains and roads. I liked the train. Everyone rolling and rocking, you know you get everything on this VIP tour.

Mae Sot was an appreciated first night stop on the trip

David. I think one was the time we spent in Thailand on the first night in Mae Sot. I loved Mae Sot and the markets.

Burmese Women in their stunning sarongs

Jean. And the third thing was the beautiful women.

Manu. The women woman and especially the ass, their wonderful ass. Okay? Little and very elegant. Well dressed. Very sexy but never vulgar. This is a big difference with Pattaya. *(laughter)*

Chris. The elegantly dressed ladies. It was mostly about how they look when they dress so nice and those very nice sarongs. They're perfectly folded and even though a lot of the are very poor, their clothes are immaculate.

. . .

Travelling slowly

Manu. For me the most important was to travel slowly and I feel very, very good because I travel very, very slow.

Water stations

Chris. One of the nice things to discover was the was the water stations. That is something that they do for travellers, everywhere else they try to make money off of travellers and see how they can exploit them, but here this is something that they do with from their heart. It was really nice to see.

Food

Tracy. The food was nice, well, except for that meal when we just arrived at Kyaikkhami. I loved discovering tealeaf salad.

Going and finishing

Areeya. I liked that I had a chance to finally go. I have a lot to do. Firstly, at the beginning, I was not sure that I should go because I have my mom and my son to look after. The house worries and the guests coming. So at the end, I put everything on my bed and then said – yes let's go.

The problem was, my passport only had five months left. So I have to run to Bangkok with only one day before we are leaving.

Then at the border another challenge. No visa.

So I was thinking should I go back because it's 3500 Thai baht, quite a lot. Finally I was very happy because I have a chance to be in this book and to learn more about how you guys travel. And what makes you enjoy it and want to keep coming back.

Chris. And the third best thing was when it was all finished because there was nothing else to worry about.

BIGGEST CHALLENGES

Humid weather, steep hills and testy immigration folk featured among the top responses to the question about the biggest challenges.

Hot weather havoc. Cycling and steep hills

Tseng. It was hot, hot, hot. Under the sun of noon. Riding is absolutely a challenge.

Manu. For me the main difficulty was to follow the main group because I'm not on the same level as everyone else.

Jeannine. Steep hills without mental preparation. When I know in advance – it's not too bad.
[Chris to Jeannine – Which hills?]

Jeannine. The six kilometres at the Myanmar and Thai border. It's difficult for me to get on and off the bike.
[David to Jeanine - And what about the journey to the border?]

Jeannine. No. no. I like it. I was interested to learn about the life of the two guys who do this drive every day to the border – two times.

Jean. I didn't like the ride out of the San Hlan village. Too steep.

Immigration officials and con artists

David. The worst for me was the immigration people. I know you laugh Manu but I was very, very, very disturbed by the man that stopped us. And then when they came and asked us what we were doing, where we were traveling- it's just not right. I think with the immigration people. I found that very stressful when the authorities came along. You weren't so concerned Manu but I have an issue with all authority. I'm terrified of policemen and teachers. I had an issue with that from my childhood.

Manu. I was not concerned about the incident with the immigration men maybe because of my long experience of revolutionary men and police repression. For me it was important that these men do not lose face.

Chow. Maybe I feel a little bit afraid when the policeman tried to try to stop us going to the village. Being with others was helpful. If I had been alone, I would have got away from the village as soon as I could.

Chris. The police and the immigration did not bother me at all. Those countries where you go like Cambodia, you will face these things and they're not actually harmful. They're not dangerous. They just want you gone. They don't want you in their area because then they have to worry about what you're doing. You're not something good. You're something they want to get rid of.

Tracy. When we were at that pagoda near Kyaikkhami, and those shifty guys tried to convince us to give them our passports - I loved the way that Areeya was so polite with them. I had to bite my tongue and not be Australian and tell them in no uncertain terms to piss off. It was really interesting thinking about the cultural nuances here. I was angry about them trying to take advantage of us. I mean, it was a small thing, but Areeya dealt with it so beautifully and appropriately.

San Hlan village

David. It was good. In a way it was also the worst one of the bad things. It was a horrible place. Yeah, for me, it was a horrible because of all this shit on the beach and the village was so poor.

Travelling slowly

Manu. Yes. I'm very, very, very slow and sometimes I feel abandoned by the group, who doesn't think of me. You don't care if I die. *(Laughter)*

Chris. I care if you die Manu. It's a big problem for me.
   (Laughter)

Language

Tseng. Because my bad English, the English listening and speaking is a challenge for me.

Food and Teahouses

Manu. Another point would be the food. In Thailand to eat is a pleasure every day. In Burma you don't have the same pleasure.

[Chatter with other expressing disagreement.]

I don't really like this food. Very Indian. But this was not important. Okay. I never had a bad stomach. So no problem.

Tracy. After Chris, Chow and I went cycling with the Dawei club we visited a tea house. I love the concept of a tea house, as a community centre, but I hate it when they pour tea into the tea cup and saucer. I hate that. And so they poured tea for Chow and for Chris into the tea cup and saucer. Yuk. And they gave us three sorts of pastries. The little samosas with curry were nice was but the other two pastries were not. But the worst thing was that, I was just trying to be very careful so that we didn't get didn't get sick. And there was a woman behind the counter who had two bits of fabric stuck up her nose. And she obviously had a cold or something. It was awful.

I like an English tea house. I love a China tea cup, and a small scone with jam and cream and just sitting in a perfectly pristine environment. And this was the complete opposite.

I remember when Les and I went to Mandalay several years back and I was so excited that teahouses were such a part of the culture and I really wanted to enjoy them. But to be honest, it's just not my cup of tea.

Morning movements

Tseng. Every day the trip begins early. And I have constipation. It makes me nervous for the morning departure on time.

[Tracy to Tseng - Me too Tseng. That's why I always carry instant porridge].

Journey to the border

David. The journey back on the last day was a challenge but and interesting one. It's something that we'll be talking about for a very long time.

Tracy. So, the adventure to the border. There was one moment, I don't know if you noticed when the truck slipped as we were approaching a bridge, and there was this gap between the bridge and the gorge. I was sure we were gone. And some of those bridges we crossed – I didn't have confidence that they were strong enough to carry us. Now that now that that journey is behind us, I can reflect upon it and laugh about it.

Recalcitrant comrades

Chris. For me probably the on this trip was dealing with the creation of the biking union. This is something that's gonna have to stop. When I say we're going to the pagoda at 5:00 – we're going to the pagoda. *(Laughter)*

[David to Chris - but what about the stress of organising all those boats?]

Chris. I do worry that it will work out the right way. But it always does. It always works out but it's stressful beforehand.

Fitting in

Areeya. I think the most challenging for me is to fit in with the group and make things as smooth as possible. It's different from when you are at our house. I know how I can help. It's harder on the trip. There are things you can't plan. Some days people can bike and other days they can't. How can I help Chris to manage this?

[Jean to Areeya - The trip was much better with you coming along.]

[David to Areeya - You have to come on every trip now.]

WORDS DESCRIBING OUR LEADER

Tseng. Chris is cordial and has the ability to solve difficulties. He also really likes cycling.

Tracy. For me, Chris is like Thor played by the movie star Chris Hemsworth. Thor has so much energy. For Chris there's no problem that can't be solved, no mountain, that can't be climbed. Because Chris doesn't panic about anything, I don't panic.

Jeannine. I agree with you Tracy. Same Same. We feel safe.

Chris. I try to look calm. I don't want everybody to panic.

Tracy. When you're cycling with Chris you are pushed beyond your comfort zone. I do things I don't normally do. I mean, people think I'm adventurous, but you know Chris, you're the one who's brave and adventurous. You talk to everybody; to the woman who was mending the fishing net and we found out that her husband had drowned. To our driver Amin, we learned about his life and about his child getting his cleft palate fixed curtesy of the UN and of the trouble he had educating his children. These are things you don't get from guidebooks.

Areeya. I must say that Chris cares for you all. There are different people, different nationalities, different strengths and different weakness. He comes up with the best way considering these things.

Jean. Chris is loved by many people. I love Chris.
[Steady on Jean]

Jeannine. These trips without Chris – would not have happened. And without these trips Jean would not be with us today. He's so happy here. He's had major health issues, and having these trips gives him inspiration– something to look forward to.

Chris. So you will make me a shrine?

David. With a spirit house so we can all pray.

Areeya. In previous years you were younger, it was easier. But now you're all old people.

David. What are you trying to say Areeya? Maybe we all need electric bikes?

Chris. No, not electric bikes. We will all ride tandems and hire people to take the front position.

Chris. Seriously though - who's up for the next cycling trip? I'm thinking China. I'm thinking Gobi desert …

PLANNING A CYCLING TRIP IN BURMA
FROM CHRIS

I have long wanted to run a bicycle tour in Myanmar. I've done many bicycle and kayaking tours in Thailand, where I live. Also, I have explored in depth, neighbouring Laos, Cambodia, Vietnam, Malaysia, Taiwan and China, yet I have never done a tour in Myanmar even though it is Thailand's closest neighbour to my home, Hidden Holiday House.

Why, do you ask, have I omitted such a convenient destination? For one, overland travel between Thailand and Myanmar had not been possible until 2015. Before 2015 a bike tour would have to start and finish at the airport in Yangon or Mandalay. Another difficulty is that several areas in Myanmar are not open to foreigners and the situation is very fluid making it difficult to know whether an area will be open when you plan to make your trip. A final issue is the limited number of foreigner approved hotels. I will expand on all these issues later but all these issues make planning a bike trip in Myanmar less obvious and more problematic than a quick glance at a map would indicate.

The long sliver of Myanmar extending south-east of Yangon squeezed between the Andaman Sea and the Tenasserim Hills which form the border between Myanmar and Thailand has always piqued my interest ever since reading the book "Siamese White" by Maurice Collis. This is where I would attempt to design an interesting bike route. It is an area inhabited by four of the eight main ethnic groups of Myanmar namely the Bamar, Mon, Kayin (Karen) and Rakhine. All have their own languages, customs and stories which makes the tour more interesting. This area is also far from the main tourist trail which includes Yangon, Mandalay, Bagan and Inle Lake. The locals along such routes are likely to be friendly and curious about us as we are about them.

I spent countless hours examining satellite photos and drawing routes along small roads and tracks far away from busy highways. I planned to run a Tough Nut tour with fitter guests where we would ride up to 100km per day and a Soft Nut tour where we would ride no more than 60km in a day. I still had many questions regarding what guesthouses/hotels we could stay at, restaurants we could eat at and interesting places we could visit. I decided to go on a bicycle scouting trip from Yangon to Dawei in Feb 2019 to answer these questions.

Cycling out from the Yangon International Airport and picking my way through the shoulder to shoulder traffic in Yangon made leaving the city not a great experience. After leaving Yangon the riding became very good . People were friendly and curious, food was quite different than in Thailand and tasty, beer was cold and cheap.

The fifth day was the biggest test of my plan. The obvious choice for traveling between Mawlamyine and Thanbyuzayat is the highway. I devised a plan to avoid the highway and visit the spectacular Yele pagoda at Kyaikkami at the same time. The plan was to cross from Mawlamyine to the very big Bilu Island, bike 25km to a small fishing village near the town of Mu Yit Ka Le, find someone with a boat and persuade him to take me on a 2 hour boat ride to Kyaikkami.

I arrived at the said fishing village and after much gesticulation and discouraging indications of "no boat" from the locals I found a fisherman with missing teeth and barely understandable Thai, who told me he could take me tomorrow. This was due to the falling tide as far as I could tell. A young sun burnt fisherman named Tun with even worse teeth and no Thai said he could take me today as he knew some rocks where we could disembark despite the low tide. After agreeing on a price and loading in my bike we took his boat on the 2 hour trip to Kyaikkami. Upon arrival all we could see were vast stretches of mudflats. We could see the rocks which Tun talked about but there was a stretch of about 100m of mud separating us from them. Tun indicated that the only way to get to the rocks was to jump off the boat and push it through the mud to the rocks. Easier said than done.

When I jumped out I immediately sank up to my waist in mud. After flapping about, I found that by making myself more horizontal than vertical I could greatly reduce the sinkage and increase my pushing power. After much time and effort we arrived at the rocks completely covered in mud. Mental note to self – when running the bike tour with guests make sure to arrange the tour dates to arrive at Kyaikkami when high tide happens at midday. This is what I love about traveling in Asia. Everything is possible. There is a solution to everything. People here are so resourceful!

Kyaikkami is a small town with a nice beach (at high tide) and a spectacular pagoda which juts out to the sea and would make a great place to spend the night on the bike tour. There is a small guesthouse as well as a large beach side hotel but both informed me that they are not "foreigner approved" so I could not stay there.

A hotel does not attain the "foreigner approved" designation by meeting a certain level of comfort or cleanliness. I have stayed in some grubby "foreigner approved" hotels in Myanmar. In order for a hotel to obtain the "foreigner approved" designation the hotel owner must do all the paper work.

I talked to a hotel owner in Mawlamyine who said that this paperwork is very time consuming as documents must be submitted to several ministries. Only hotels that expect several foreign guests will bother to do this paperwork which means that you will normally find "foreigner approved" hotels in tourist centers or in places where foreigners work. A place like Kyaikkami has very few foreign visitors so the hotels here do not bother getting foreigner certified. I cannot help to think that more foreigner visitors would come to this beautiful spot if there was a place for them to stay so it is a bit of the "chicken and egg" problem.

Planning a cycling trip in Burma 137

No choice but to push on another 26km to the next place with "foreigner approved" accommodation.

On the sixth day I arrived in the town of Ye. I plan to have a rest day here during the tour with guests and would like to plan an easy bike ride to see the countryside around here. My first choice is a ride to Juan Yua village to the east of Ye and taking a boat from there a short distance up the Ye river. Upon talking about my plan with people in Ye I found out that this is not possible due to some recent skirmishes in that area between the Tatmadaw (Myanmar national army) and the Karen Liberation Army (KLA). This is a common occurrence in Myanmar. Various ethnic groups have taken up arms against the national army in the hope of carving out an independent state. A ceasefire agreement has been signed in recent years but flareups are common and can impact your tour planning. Many areas in Myanmar are still considered too dangerous or too sensitive and are completely off limits to foreigners.

The route between the towns Ye and Dawei is 165km with only one village in between which has a guesthouse which is "foreigner approved" at roughly the half way point. This will make for a nice ride for the Tough Nut tour but it the distance is too long for the Soft Nut version. I will need to arrange transport in Ye for my group and bicycles. Luckily it is easily done through our guesthouse in Ye.

While looking for information on the internet about the areas we will pass through I came across an article talking about a community based tourism project set up in the fishing village of San Hlan 30km from Dawei. The accommodation is simple. The food is prepared by the villagers and the views are incredible. I really like this type stay as you can get close to the locals and see how they live. As almost all places we stay at on this tour are in towns this will be a nice change of pace for the group.

ACKNOWLEDGMENTS

This book was made possible by the contributions of the following members of the Soft Nut Bike Troupe.

Chris (M) Canadian. Curious. Courageous. Runs Hidden Holiday House with Areeya.

Areeya (F) Thai. Tour photographer. Runs Hidden Holiday House with Chris.

Manu (M) French. Revolutionary. History professor (retired). Lover of South-East Asia.

Jean (M) French. Maths teacher (retired). Bon vivant.

Jeannine (F) French. German teacher (retired). Bonne vivante.

Chow (M) Malaysian. Survivor of the Tough Nut Bike Tour.

Tseng (M) Taiwanese. Maths teacher. Enjoyed this 2nd trip with Chris with all of its surprises.

David (M) English. Blissfully retired from overseas trade. Cycling and adventure enthusiast.

Teerayud (M) Thai. Business man. Food lover.

Soft Nut Tour troupe: From left: Chow, Teerayud, Manu, Chris, Areeya, Jeannine, David, Tseng and Jean

ABOUT TRACY STANLEY

I loved the adventures of *The Secret Seven* as a child: a small troupe solving mysteries together, often on their bicycles. Their exploits inspired my career in foreign lands and interest in understanding what makes a great team. I love listening to people with diverse life stories. My friends say that I am imaginative and tenacious, although my husband would hasten to add 'untidy'.

Following a corporate career in human resource management and organisational change working within travel, technology, government, financial services, mining, education and health sectors, I am now a consultant and writer. My other books include

Engagement Whisperer: A quieter and more collaborative approach to inspiring your team team

. . .

Creativity Cycling: Help your team solve complex problems with creative tools, co-written with creativity expert, Barbara Wilson

Always keen to learn, I've acquired a few qualifications including a Master of Business (Research), MBA and a PhD. My doctoral research considered how work environments impact on creative behaviours and employee engagement.

Apart from writing books, I blog. You can read my musings on life in organisations at

http://tjstanley.com/articles/

You can also find me on the following **social media channels.**

Facebook https://www.facebook.com/Engagewhisperer/

Twitter @tjstanley64

LinkedIn https://www.linkedin.com/in/tracystanley1/

Bookbub https://www.bookbub.com/authors/tracy-stanley

. . .

Pinterest https://www.pinterest.com.au/tjstanley64/

YouTube https://www.youtube.com/channel/UC98owLf5k5GWEjWGgus-7vQ

Goodreads https://www.goodreads.com/author/show/18989774.Tracy_Stanley

Instagram https://www.instagram.com/tjstanley64/?hl=en

I write a monthly newsletter about what I've been learning about organisational change, creativity, innovation and employee engagement. You can read the most recent ones at the link below and sign up by popping your email in the box.

http://tjstanley.com/newsletters-learning-creativity/

You can find me online at: www.tjstanley.com

ABOUT LES STANLEY

I was, as Groucho Marx said, born at an early age, in London (England). My parents moved to the Kent coast when I was seven. I caught up with them a year or so later.

My school days were unremarkable. Some were marked but usually very badly. The only subject I had any affinity with was English and this was mainly because my parents both spoke it, often at the same time.

My career has taken many turns, dips and troughs, a few false starts and even one or two emergency landings. However, it seems I was destined for an eventual career in the travel industry.

Following a failed attempt to make my fortune as a driving instructor, I joined British Airways as a Sales Agent where I stayed for 4 years before emigrating to Australia after marrying local girl Tracy. Fortunately for me this coincided with the rise of the CRS (Computer Reservations System) which later morphed in to GDS (Global Distribution System).

I worked in Australia for a company called Galileo and in Europe and Asia for Amadeus. Both companies offered similar products and, obviously, both were best when I was an employee.

I retired from the corporate treadmill 2 years ago and I'm now officially an author.

My first book is **My Brother's Bicycle**.

It describes a journey of contemplation and misadventure as I attempt, mostly unsuccessfully to re-live a bicycle trip I first embarked on as a fresh-faced 20-year-old

More than 40 years ago I headed south with a guy I met at Liverpool Street station in London. Enfield to Athens on a tandem. They said it couldn't be done. For the re-run I was better prepared, or so I thought. But as it turned out it didn't really matter.

. . .

My Brother's Bicycle is a story of (limited) endurance, survival (over boredom) and indomitable spirit.

Please join my newsletter for monthly tales of my travels.
   www.lesstanley.com

I'm also on LinkedIn
   https://www.linkedin.com/in/les-stanley-3969731/

Here we are together near Kirra Beach , Queensland in Australia

ABOUT HIDDEN HOLIDAY HOUSE

Hidden Holiday House is a family run guest house with four guest rooms. It is located on the bank of the Ta Jin river in the district of Nakhon Chaisri. The owners Areeya and Chris will treat you as part of their family. This region has not yet been discovered by many international tourists but is popular with Thai weekend travellers. It is famous for the quality of fruits and rice it produces and most people here are still pursuing a traditional way of life as they have been doing for generations. Hidden Holiday House is a one hour drive from Bangkok making it a perfect location for a weekend getaway.

Chris is an avid cyclist and kayaker and many of his guests use Hidden Holiday House as the base for their cycling holiday in Thailand. You can rent one of his bicycles or bring your own. Chris can arrange a taxi to transport you and your bike from the airport to Hidden Holiday House. Several regular guests (including myself and Les) leave their bicycles at his place for the convenience of their annual cycling vacations. Chris can also advise you on your self-guided adventure or organise a bicycle of kayak tour for you.

At Hidden Holiday House near Huay Plu

About Hidden Holiday House

http://www.hiddenholidayhouse.com/index.php/en/homehhh-en-gb

FAVOURITE FOODS AND SNACKS

Nescafe iced coffee
Coconut juice (fresh)
Avocado smoothie
Pumpkin and sunflower seeds
Deep fried broad beans
Peanuts
Spring roles
Samosas

Recipe for Tea Leaf salad (Lahpet)

Delicious traditional Burmese salad prepared with fermented tea leaves.

INGREDIENTS

Pickled or fermented Tea Leaves
1 cup dried green tea leaves
1 cup finely chopped cabbage
3 scallions (spring onions) finely chopped
1 bunch cilantro (coriander leaves) finely chopped
1 (1-inch) piece ginger, peeled and finely chopped
2 cloves garlic, crushed
½ Thai chili pepper, finely chopped (optional)
Zest of 2 limes
Juice of 2 limes
1 cup vegetable oil

For the Lahpet Thoke (Fermented Tea Leaf Salad)

¾ cup fermented tea leaves, drained from oil
2 tablespoons toasted sesame seeds
3 tablespoons roasted peanuts
1 tablespoon fried garlic (fried, thinly sliced garlic)
1 tablespoon fried yellow split peas (after soaking overnight)
1 tomato, sliced in thin wedges
2 tablespoons dried shrimp, soaked in water for 10 minutes and drained (optional)
1 cup shredded cabbage
Juice of 1 lime
1 teaspoon sugar

1 teaspoon fish sauce
1 tablespoon garlic oil

INSTRUCTIONS

1. Infuse the dried green tea leaves in hot water for 10 minutes.
2. Discard the liquid (or drink it), and cover tea leaves with lukewarm water. Drain and press on the leaves thoroughly to get rid of bitter juices. Repeat this step two more times.
3. After discarding the liquid again, add cold water, and let the leaves soak for at least 2 hours (or overnight).
4. Drain out excess liquid thoroughly by squeezing the leaves one handful at a time. Then, finely chopped the leaves in a blender or food processor.
5. Mix the drained chopped tea leaves with shredded cabbage, cilantro, scallions, as well as ginger, garlic, and Thai chili (optional).
6. Finally, sprinkle lime zest, pour in lime juice, and mix well.
7. Place the mixture in a glass or earthenware container and cover tightly.
8. Let the mixture ferment at room temperature for 3 to 4 days.
9. Add 1 cup (250ml) of vegetable oil to the fermented tea leaves to preserve them.

THEN
>   Mix all the ingredients
>   Drizzle with garlic oil to finish.

Recipe from website below with endorsement from **Soe Thein,** author of Burmese cuisine food blog Lime and Cilantro.

https://www.196flavors.com/burma-lahpet-thoke-fermented-tea-leaf-salad/

REFERENCES AND FURTHER READING

This is Burma and it will be quite unlike any land you know about. Rudyard Kipling (*Letters from the East* in 1898)

Collis, M. (2016) Siamese White, Faber & Faber

Dermott-Powell, Eric (1996), War cemeteries in Burma : 1939-1945 : names and particulars of British Forces buried in the Thanbyuzayat War Cemetery, E. Dermott-Powell, ISBN 978-1-875609-29-1

Kipling, R. (2000). Rudyard Kipling. Sterling Publishing Company, Inc.

Larkin, E. (2011). Finding George Orwell in Burma. Granta Books

. . .

Ollard, Richard (1984). Pepys: a biography (First published 1974 ed.). Oxford: Oxford University Press

Pinney, T. (Ed.). (1995). *The Letters of Rudyard Kipling: Volume 3: 1900-10*. Springer

Reference - Wright, Colin. "Maulmein. Great pagoda [Kyaik-Than-Lan pagoda]". www.bl.uk. Retrieved 5 February 2019.

http://www.kiplingsociety.co.uk/rg_mandalay1.htm

Web Site references

Travel Fish
    https://www.travelfish.org/
    https://allpointseast.com/blog/tour-info/burma-myanmar/burma-quite-unlike-any-land-you-know-about/
    https://yourthaiguide.com/real-name-of-bangkok/

About Myanmar
    https://en.wikipedia.org/wiki/Mae_Sot_District
    https://en.wikipedia.org/wiki/Anglo-Burmese_people

Driving on which side of the road reference
    https://www.theguardian.com/travel/2016/jan/17/burmese-days-george-orwell-burma-myanmar

https://www.irrawaddy.com/specials/on-this-day/day-myanmar-started-driving-right.html

Ethnic groups in Myanmar

https://en.wikipedia.org/wiki/List_of_ethnic_groups_in_Myanmar

PHOTOS FROM THE TOUR

Bumping into David and Chow in Mae Sot

In Mae Sot

Photos from the tour

Tuk tuk driver and seller of amulets

Window shopping in Mae Sot. Love these fabrics

Photos from the tour

Professional bike cleaners

Departure day Mae Sot. Photo out front of T Guest House.

Photos from the tour

And so the tour begins

At the border

Lunch stop in village of Ein Du

This family were also having lunch

Photos from the tour

Areeya taking photo from roof top in Golden Palace Hotel, Hpa An

View from Golden Palace

Different view from the Golden Place

Hpa An town centre

Exploring Hpa An

Chris and Areeya discuss tactics

Heading off to explore Hpa An

Riding near Zwegabin mountains near Hpa An

Photos from the tour

Zwegabin mountains, no people

Pagoda, pagoda

Pagoda market

Kyauk Kalat Pagoda

Photos from the tour

Children playing tag at Kyauk Kalat Pagoda

Pagoda with ducks

Salween River, Hpa An

Sunset cruise

Photos from the tour

Fabulous evening cruise in Hpa An

Relaxing on the Salween river

Watching bats exit their caves

On the road again

Emerging from Saddar Cave

Woman selling tortoises and fish for making merit

And a lady walked past with her pigs at Saddar Cave

Two little boys near their parents market stall at Saddar Cave

Photos from the tour

Stationary monks

Cruising around Saddar Cave

Another market

Roadside dwellings

Birds

Buddhas in the sun

Photos from the tour

Chow and Areeya stop to chat to a farmer

The bikes take a rest

Jean Jeannine and Manu on their bikes

Narrow boat rides

Photos from the tour

Observing the production of rubber bands

Chicken shopping at the local markets

Reclining Buddha and location for formation of Soft Nut Union

Photos from the tour

Temples and pagodas at Mawlamyine

Character on right straight out of Tom Hanks film Big

Taking in the view at Mawlamyine made famous by George Orwell

Morning markets surrounding a pagoda

First boat ride for today

Bikes on a boat

Photos from the tour

Another boat ride

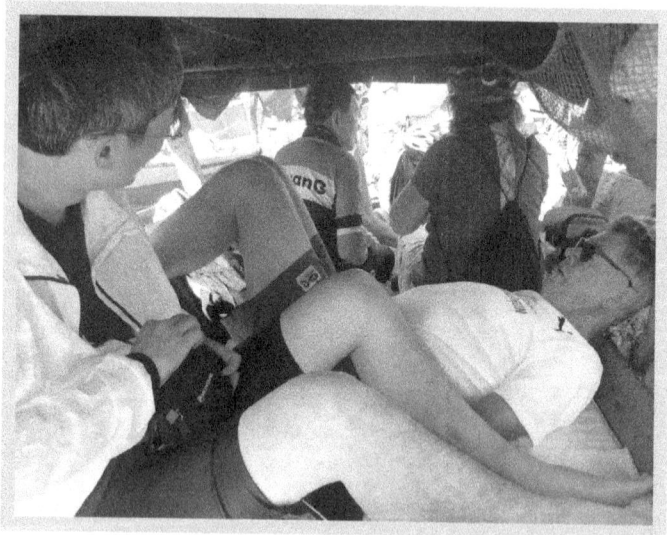

Plenty of room on top

Photos from the tour

On the upper deck

Captain and his mate

Disembarking at Kyaikkhami

Taking rest while Chris negotiates portage fees

Monks collecting their morning alms

Ladies selling food while train stops at Thanbyuzayat

Quickly loading our bikes into luggage carriage at Thanbyuzayat

Half bearded Buddha

Chris repairing Manu's broken brakes

Young boy acting as translator for the police

Village supporters

At Banana Mountain near Ye

Which one's Jeannine?

Chris' shortcut through the burning rubbish tip

Manu leading the way to Bin Le Wa beach

Photos from the tour

At Bin Le Wa Beach

Beach snoozing spot

Photos from the tour

Loading the bikes and panniers for journey to San Hlan

Passing through a checkpoint

Photos from the tour

Girls working hard bringing produce from the boats to the storage houses

Young boys playing on the sand

Chris chatting to a lady mending fishing nets at San Hlan

View across San Hlan bay

Photos from the tour

View from community owned guest house at San Hlan

Fishing boats at San Hlan

Chris checks the bikes

Guest house at San Hlan

Jeannine checking out the mosquito nets

Room with a view, San Hlan

Getting into the truck to get a ride up the hill out of San Hlan

En route to Dawei

Wooden house, Dawei

Hindu Thaipusam Festival, Dawei

Not a real elephant

Photos from the tour

In Dawei Main Street

Fabric shopping in Dawei

Photos from the tour

Dawei Cycling Club ride

Packing the bikes for the drive to the Thai/Myanmar border

Border town of Htee Kee

Getting ready to ride through no man's land into Thailand

www.ingramcontent.com/pod-product-compliance
Lightning Source LLC
Chambersburg PA
CBHW050309010526
44107CB00055B/2174